INVESTIGATIVE REPORT WRITING *WORKBOOK*

Designed for use with: The Investigative Report Writing Manual for Law Enforcement and Security Personnel

Police and Fire Publishing
1800 N Bristol St, Ste C408
Santa Ana, Ca. 92707

e-mail: steve@policeandfirepublishing.com
www.policeandfirepublishing.com

ISBN: 978-1-936986-14-9

QR (Quick Response) Codes

http://www.policeandfirepublishing.com

QR (Quick Response) codes incorporate advanced technology to deliver a reality-based application beyond the textbook. The subject matter "comes to life" through a video clip, complete with the sights and sounds unique to each chapter; each QR code offers a broader perspective of the material being taught and a better understanding of how it is applied in the field.

QR codes can be quickly accessed with a cell phone and are tailor-made for quick and easy linking to content on smart phones. Simply point the phone's camera at the QR code you wish to scan. There are a number of apps in the iPhone App Store that can read QR codes, including the free QR Reader. Most Android phones and Blackberries read the codes right out of the box, as can newer Nokia headsets. For older Androids and Blackberries, download free QR reader applications. Windows Mobile users can download Quick Marks.

Chapter 1 - <u>HOW REPORTS ARE USED</u>

<u>SIX PRIMARY WAYS THAT REPORTS ARE UTILIZED</u>

1. _____
2. _____
3. _____
4. _____
5. _____
6. _____

<u>WHAT MAKES AN EXCELLENT REPORT – SIX BASIC AND NECESSARY QUALITIES</u>

<u>LIST AND DEFINE EACH</u>

1. _____
2. _____
3. _____
4. _____
5. _____
6. _____

ADDITIONAL CHRACTERISTICS OF A WELL-WRITTEN REPORT

<u>LIST AND DEFINE EACH</u>

1. _____
2. _____
3. _____

<u>MOST COMMON UTILIZATION OF REPORTS</u>

<u>LIST AND BRIEFLY DESCRIBE EACH</u>

1. _____
2. _____
3. _____
4. _____

REVIEWING AUDIENCE

1. _____
2. _____
3. _____
4. _____
5. _____
6. _____

TYPES OF REPORTS

1. _____
   _____
2. _____
   _____
3. _____
   _____
4. _____
   _____
5. _____
   _____
6. _____
   _____
7. _____
   _____
8. _____
   _____
9. _____
   _____
10. _____
    _____
11. _____
    _____

Chapter 2 – <u>INTERVIEWING AND NOTE TAKING</u>

<u>COMPLETE THE STATEMENT</u>

ALWAYS REMEMBER: IF YOU DON'T ASK SPECIFIC QUESTIONS, YOU PROBABLY WON'T GET _____

<u>GENERAL RULES CONCERNING INTERVIEWS</u>

1. _____
2. _____
3. _____

<u>NOTE TAKING TIPS</u>

1. _____
2. _____
3. _____
4. _____
5. _____
6. _____
   _____

<u>CONDUCTING THE INTERVIEW</u>

<u>LIST THE PRIMARY STEPS FOR CONDUCTING THE INTERVIEW</u>

1. _____
2. _____
3. _____

WHO, WHAT, WHEN, WHY, WHERE, AND HOW

LIST FIVE QUESTIONS FOR EACH CATEGORY

WHO

    1. _____
    2. _____
    3. _____
    4. _____
    5. _____

WHAT

    1. _____
    2. _____
    3. _____
    4. _____
    5. _____

WHY

    1. _____
    2. _____
    3. _____
    4. _____
    5. _____

WHERE

    1. _____
    2. _____
    3. _____
    4. _____
    5. _____

HOW

    1. _____
    2. _____
    3. _____
    4. _____
    5. _____

OBSTACLES TO OVERCOME IN INTERVIEWS

SIGNS THAT THE VICTIM IS IN CRISIS

1. _____
2. _____
3. _____
4. _____
5. _____
6. _____
7. _____
8. _____
9. _____

EXTREME RESPONSES

1. _____
2. _____
3. _____
4. _____
5. _____

GENERAL GUIDELINES FOR VICTIM INTERVIEWS

1. _____
2. _____
3. _____
4. _____
5. _____
6. _____
7. _____
8. _____
9. _____
10. _____
11. _____
12. _____
13. _____

GUIDELINES FOR INTERVIEWING CHILDREN

1. _____
_____
_____

2. _____
_____
_____

3. _____
_____
_____

4. _____
_____
_____

5. _____
_____
_____

6. _____
_____
_____

7. _____
_____
_____

8. _____
_____
_____

9. _____
_____
_____

10. _____
_____
_____

11. _____
_____
_____

12. _____
_____
_____

EVALUATING DEMEANOR AND MENTAL CAPACITY

LIST EIGHT QUESTIONS USED TO DETERMINE MENTAL CAPACITY

1. _____
2. _____
3. _____
4. _____
5. _____
6. _____
7. _____
8. _____

LIST SIX QUESTIONS TO ESTABLISH A SUSPECT'S DEMEANOR

1. _____
2. _____
3. _____
4. _____
5. _____
6. _____

DEFINE KEY ELEMENTS IN INTERVIEWING ABUSED SPOUSES

_____
_____
_____
_____

LIST SEVERAL TIPS FOR INTERVIEWING A CHILD WHO HAS BEEN MOLESTED

_____
_____
_____
_____

DESCRIBE OPTIONS IN DEALING WITH A LANGUAGE BARRIER

_____
_____

LIST THREE OPTIONS FOR DEALING WITH A DEAF INDIVIDUAL

1. _____
2. _____
3. _____

WHAT IS THE MOST IMPORTANT ELEMENT WHEN DEALING WITH AN INDIVIDUAL WHO IS MENTALLY CHALLENGED

BE _____ AND TRY NOT TO GET _____

EXPLAIN WHY THE ABOVE STATEMENT IS SO IMPORTANT

_____
_____

EXPLAIN WHY IT IS IMPORTANT TO LOCK A VICTIM AND/OR WITNESS INTO A STATEMENT

_____
_____

EXPLAIN WHY IT IS SO IMPORTANT TO AVOID "AUTO PILOT" WHEN WRITING REPORTS

_____
_____
_____
_____

LIST KEY ELEMENTS NEEDED FOR PROPER CONTACT INFORMATION AND WHY IT IS IMPORTANT TO DOCUMENT THESE

_____
_____
_____
_____

DESCRIBE PRODEDURE FOR READING A SUSPECT MIRANDA RIGHTS AND HOW TIMING CAN AFFECT THE OUTCOME OF AN ARREST

_____

_____

_____

_____

THE REPORT

An officer writes a report and makes the _____ or the _____ follows up on the information and makes the arrest.

The report is delivered to _____. A prosecutor will review the case and determine if there is enough evidence to convince a jury of twelve the person is guilty.

ARRAIGNMENT

If the case is filed, the arrestee is entitled to an arraignment within ____ hours of their arrest and a preliminary hearing within ____ calendar days.

PRE-TRIAL

There will be pre-trials in which the _____ and _____ try to forge a deal to close the case.

MOTIONS

A common delay tactic by the _____ is to file a Motion to Suppress Evidence Hearing. This is similar to a preliminary hearing in which the officer will testify with only a judge present. The judge will determine if the _____ can be used at trial.

TRIAL

If a deal cannot be made the case will proceed to a _____ by a judge or jury. A jury is comprised of _____ people who must unanimously decide on a guilty or not guilty verdict; otherwise it is declared a hung jury and mistrial. If a mistrial occurs the _____ decides whether or not to retry the case.

POLLING THE JURY

Polling the jury is a term for _____ .

AUDIO AND VIDEO TAPE RECORDING

LIST THE FIVE PIECES OF INFORMATION TO ALWAYS INCLUDE ON THE TAPE

1. _____
2. _____
3. _____
4. _____
5. _____

ISSUES WITH RECORDINGS

Broken or dead space in the tape needs to be _____ .

EXPLAIN THE PREVIOUS ANSWER

_____
_____
_____
_____

ANTICIPATING DEFENSES

Experience will help you with closing defenses, but _____ can place you ahead of the experience curve. There will be cases that will invite hard questioning by a defense attorney through no fault of your own. It may even be caused by exculpatory evidence you included in your report. You of course should have done everything in your power to refute anything exculpatory, but simply report _____ even if they hurt your case.

Always tell the _____ even if you can feel the case leaning toward an acquittal.

One of the most common complaints made by District Attorneys about police reports is

_____
_____

Chapter 3 – <u>DESCRIPTIONS OF SUSPECTS AND PROPERTY</u>

<u>IDENTIFYING THE PARTIES</u>

<u>LIST AND DESCRIBE THE FIVE PARTIES OF INVOLVEMENT</u>

1. _____
2. _____
3. _____
4. _____
5. _____

<u>SUSPECT DESCRIPTION CHECKLIST</u>

<u>LIST AND BRIEFLY DESCRIBE THE 17 MAJOR ITEMS ON THE SUSPECT DESCRIPTION CHECKLIST</u>

1. _____
2. _____
3. _____
4. _____
5. _____
6. _____
7. _____
8. _____
9. _____
10. _____
11. _____
12. _____
13. _____
14. _____
15. _____
16. _____
17. _____

PROPERTY

LIST FIVE VITAL DETAILS FOR A PROPERTY DESCRIPTION

1. _____
2. _____
3. _____
4. _____
5. _____

LIST SIX VITAL DETAILS FOR DOCUMENTING STOLEN JEWELRY

1. _____
2. _____
3. _____
4. _____
5. _____
6. _____

ALSO BE SURE TO ASK FOR

1. _____
2. _____
3. _____

LIST SIX VITAL DETAILS FOR DOCUMENTING A STOLEN FIREARM

1. _____
2. _____
3. _____
4. _____
5. _____
6. _____

RECORDING THE DOLLAR VALUE OF THE LOSS

Note the value based upon the _____ provided by the victim. Ask for receipts, etc. If the victim doesn't know, you can generally make an educated guess. A general rule to follow to estimate value of used property is to estimate what the item would bring at a _____. When the victim has no idea of the value of an item and you can't reasonably come up with a loss amount, consider using various resources to obtain that information. For instance, a victim has had an antique watch stolen but the victim has no idea what the watch would be worth. By calling a local _____ and describing the item, you would probably be able to come up with an approximate value of the item which would be better than guessing its value. Another resource you can use to help you get approximate values on items would be the local _____, which would help in locating appraisers and local dealers that would be able to assist you.

Items that carry no value are _____.

For commercial thefts, use the _____ of the stolen items, not the retail price.

PROPERTY DAMAGE

Do not forget to include the value of _____ that has been damaged as a result of the criminal act. For example, a car window that has been smashed in an auto burglary is also a _____ to the victim, besides the stereo that was taken during the burglary. Likewise, a house window or door that was pried or broken during the burglar's entry into the residence is a _____ to the victim. These items should be recorded/listed as _____ property, with a dollar value assigned, and should be mentioned in the narrative. _____ is being more frequently required as part of a sentence, however failing to _____ these losses could jeopardize restitution being required.

VEHICLES

LIST THE SEVEN PRIMARY ITEMS ON A VEHICLE THEFT REPORT

1. _____
2. _____
3. _____
4. _____
5. _____
6. _____
7. _____

MAKE SURE TO INCLUDE THE FOLLOWING SIX ITEMS IN YOUR REPORT

1. _____
2. _____
3. _____
4. _____
5. _____
6. _____

DESCRIBING BUILDINGS AND LOCATIONS

It can be very helpful to your reader if he/she knows what type of physical environment (e.g., residential area, commercial district, etc.) the crime occurred in.   Crimes such as burglaries and robberies should include a description of the _____ and _____.

When describing locations or buildings, provide as much _____ as possible. For instance, _____ can be described by approximate square footage, number of stories, having an attached garage, alarm system, etc.   Provide information about _____ or out-of-the-ordinary circumstances such as a flood control channel or railroad nearby. Such descriptions are best placed at the _____ of the report so the reader can envision the setting.

Most _____ tend to be located in commercial or industrial areas. Provide as much _____ about the specific location (address; major intersection; adjacent businesses; etc.) and the general location, commercial or industrial area; primary industry in the area, if there is one; predominant type of buildings/ structures, if applicable - for example, refinery structures, large warehouses, retail outlets, restaurant area) of the business, and a detailed _____ of it.

COLLECTION OF EVIDENCE

LIST THE FIVE KEY COMPONENTS OF THE CHAIN OF EVIDENCE

1. _____
2. _____
3. _____
4. _____
5. _____

These are issues and concerns that may very well come up in court, so you will need to make sure that your record is _____ and _____.

Chapter 4 – <u>PRELIMINARY INVESTIGATIONS AND CRIMES THAT JUST OCCURED</u>

<u>LIST THE EIGHT COMPONENTS OF A PRELIMINARY INVESTIGATION</u>

1. _____
2. _____
3. _____
4. _____
5. _____
6. _____
7. _____
8. _____

<u>CRIME BROADCAST</u>

<u>LIST THE NINE CRUCIAL TYPES OF IDENTIFYING DATA</u>

1. _____
2. _____
3. _____
4. _____
5. _____
6. _____
7. _____
8. _____
9. _____

In cases where a crime has just occurred, it is critical that the first officer on the scene quickly obtain information for a crime broadcast. Trying to obtain the information the typical way would _____. Information must be obtained promptly if the police officers in the field are to catch a suspect who might still be in the general area, or does not have the time to flee a "safe" distance from the crime scene.

As soon as possible upon arrival at the scene, you should quickly obtain the information needed for a broadcast, such as suspect information, including _____, _____, _____, _____, _____, and _____.

Once the necessary information is given out over the radio, go back to the person(s) you originally interviewed, and using the _____, _____, _____ method, re-interview them to obtain a complete picture of what occurred. As a result of re-interviewing the parties, you may very well obtain additional information that needs to be added to the _____.

Chapter 5 – <u>A REVIEW OF GRAMMAR, PUNCTUATION AND SYNTAX</u>

<u>DEFINE GRAMMAR</u>

_____

_____

<u>DEFINE SYNTAX</u>

_____

_____

<u>DEFINE PUNCTUATION</u>

_____

_____

<u>GRAMMAR – PARTS OF SPEECH</u>

<u>DEFINE ADJECTIVE</u>

_____

_____

<u>DEFINE ADVERB</u>

_____

_____

<u>DEFINE ANTECEDENT</u>

_____

_____

DEFINE CLAUSE

_____

_____

DEFINE CONJUNCTION

_____

_____

DEFINE INTERJECTION

_____

_____

DEFINE MODIFIER

_____

_____

DEFINE NOUN

_____

_____

DEFINE OBJECT

_____

_____

DEFINE PREPOSITION

_____

_____

DEFINE PRONOUN

_____

_____

DEFINE SENTENCE

_____

_____

DEFINE SUBJECT

_____

_____

DEFINE VERB

_____

_____

THE STATEMENTS BELOW ARE _____ TENSE

1) Lie on the grass until the paramedics get here.

2) The suspect told the victim to lie down and be quiet.

3) Lie down and go to sleep.

THE STATEMENTS BELOW ARE _____ TENSE

1) The victim lay there until the paramedics arrived.

2) The suspect lay in wait for 3 hours until the victim finally got home.

THE STATEMENT BELOW CONTAINS A _____ PARTICIPLE

1) We found the gun lying on the covered ledge, where the suspect said he left it.

THE STATEMENTS BELOW CONTAIN A _____ PARTICIPLE

1) We found the gun on the ledge, where it had lain since the suspect left it there 20 years ago.

2) If the suspect had not confessed, the body could have lain in the cave forever and never been found.

LABEL THE FOLLOWING ACCORDINGLY (PAST OR PRESENT TENSE)

I laid the evidence bag on the counter so the clerk could pick it up and store it. _____

Lay the gun on the ground. _____

I like to lay my head on a pillow when I sleep. _____

Watch the suspect closely as she lays the bomb on the ground and steps back. _____

She laid the gun on the table when I told her to, and then she stepped away. _____

LABEL THE FOLLOWING ACCORDINGLY (PAST OR PRESENT PARTICIPLE)

I like laying the facts out chronologically when possible so the report is easier to follow._____

The suspects have laid a trail of misleading evidence. _____

SYNTAX - SENTENCE STRUCTURE / CONSTRUCTION

DEFINE SENTENCE FRAGMENT

_____
_____

DEFINE RUN-ON SENTENCE

_____
_____

DEFINE MISPLACED MODIFIER

_____
_____

THE DIFFERENCE BETWEEN "RECOGNIZE" AND "IDENTIFY"

To _____ implies a prior knowledge or experience of or with the person, place, thing, or sensation you are talking about. You can't "recognize" or recall someone or something without previously having seen or interacted with the person, been to the particular place, experienced the particular sensation, touched the particular object, etc.

To _____ someone or something means that you compare that person, place or thing to a standard, to a definition, or to a description. Depending on how similar the person, place, or thing is to the standard or definition or description, you can say that his, her, or its identity has been established. You have shown or proved the sameness of the person, place, or thing with the standard, definition, or description.

PUNCTUATION

PERIODS ARE USED

1. _____
2. _____
3. _____

DON'T USE PERIODS

1. _____
2. _____
3. _____

THE COLON IS USED

1. _____
2. _____

THE COMMA IS USED

1. _____
2. _____
3. _____
4. _____

THE SEMI-COLON IS USED

1. _____

THE APOSTROPHE IS USED

1. _____
2. _____

THE QUOTATION MARK IS USED

1. _____
2. _____
3. _____
4. _____
5. _____

THE DASH IS USED

1. _____

THE SLASH IS USED

1. _____

PARENTHESES ARE USED

1. _____
2. _____
3. _____

THE HYPHEN IS USED

1. _____
2. _____
3. _____
4. _____
5. _____

Chapter 6 – <u>SLANG, JARGON, ACRONYMS AND ABBREVIATIONS</u>

<u>DEFINE SLANG</u>

_____

_____

<u>DEFINE JARGON</u>

_____

_____

<u>DEFINE ACRONYMS</u>

_____

_____

<u>DEFINE INITIALS</u>

_____

_____

<u>DEFINE ABBREVIATIONS</u>

_____

_____

Chapter 7 – <u>WRITING THE REPORT</u>

<u>DEFINE ACTIVE VOICE</u>

_____

_____

<u>DEFINE PASSIVE VOICE</u>

_____

_____

<u>DEFINE FIRST PERSON</u>

_____

_____

<u>DEFINE BLOCK PRINTING AND THE ADVANTAGE OF USING IT</u>

_____

_____

<u>IDENTIFY AND DEFINE BOTH REPORT WRITING STYLES</u>

1. _____
   _____
   _____
   _____

2. _____
   _____
   _____
   _____

1. **<u>DEFINE PARAPHRASING</u>**

   _____

   _____

2. **DEFINE QUOTING**

    _____
    _____

3. **EXPLAIN THE ADVANTAGES AND DISADVANTAGES OF EACH**

    _____
    _____
    _____
    _____
    _____
    _____
    _____

LENGTHY REPORTS

THREE REASONS FOR WRITING A SYNOPSIS AND USING A LEGEND

1. _____
2. _____
3. _____

LIST EIGHT TIPS FOR DISCOVERING ERRORS

1. _____
2. _____
3. _____
4. _____
5. _____
6. _____
7. _____
8. _____

LIST THE SIX STEPS ON THE FINAL CHECKLIST

1. _____
2. _____
3. _____
4. _____
5. _____
6. _____

Chapter 8 – <u>REPORT WRITING RESPONSIBILITIES FOR SUPERVISORS</u>

<u>SUMMARIZE THE FOLLOWING AREAS OF REPORT WRITING RESPONSIBLITIES FOR SUPERVISORS</u>

<u>WHY REPORT WRITING PROBLEMS EXIST</u>

_____
_____
_____

<u>MECHANICAL ERRORS</u>

_____
_____
_____

<u>CONTENT PROBLEMS</u>

_____
_____
_____
_____

<u>READING SKILLS</u>

_____
_____
_____

<u>SPELLING</u>

_____
_____
_____
_____

COMPUTERS

_____
_____
_____
_____

SAMPLE REPORTS

_____
_____
_____
_____

TRAINING OFFICERS

_____
_____
_____
_____

DO'S AND DON'TS

_____
_____
_____
_____

FINAL ETHICAL CONSIDERATIONS

_____
_____
_____
_____

Chapter 9 – <u>INVESTIGATIVE CHECKLISTS</u>

<u>LIST THE NINE GENERAL REMINDERS</u>

1. _____
2. _____
3. _____
4. _____
5. _____
6. _____
7. _____
8. _____
9. _____

<u>ARREST BY PRIVATE PERSON INVESTIGATION CHECKLIST</u>

1. _____
2. _____
3. _____
4. _____
5. _____
6. _____
7. _____
8. _____
9. _____
10. _____

DRIVING UNDER THE INFLUENCE ARREST INVESTIGATION CHECKLIST

1. _____
   _____
   _____

2. _____
   _____
   _____

DUI BEHAVIOR WITNESSED BY THE OFFICER CHECKLIST

1. _____
   _____
   _____

2. _____
   _____
   _____

3. _____
   _____
   _____

4. _____
   _____
   _____

5. _____
   _____
   _____

6. _____
   _____
   _____

7. _____
   _____
   _____

8. _____
   _____
   _____

9. _____
   _____
   _____

DOMESTIC VIOLENCE INVESTIGATION CHECKLIST

1. _____
   _____
   _____

2. _____
   _____
   _____

3. _____
   _____
   _____

4. _____
   _____
   _____

5. _____
   _____
   _____

6. _____
   _____
   _____

7. _____
   _____
   _____

8. _____
   _____
   _____

9. _____
   _____
   _____

10. _____
    _____
    _____

MALICIOUS MISCHIEF INVESTIGATION CHECKLIST

1. _____
   _____
   _____

2. _____
   _____
   _____

3. _____
   _____

4. _____
   _____
   _____

5. _____
   _____
   _____

ROBBERY AND GRAND THEFT INVESTIGATION CHECKLIST

1. _____
   _____
   _____

2. _____
   _____
   _____

3. _____
   _____
   _____

4. _____
   _____
   _____

5. _____
   _____
   _____

6. _____
   _____
   _____

7. _____
   _____
   _____

8. _____
   _____
   _____

9. _____
   _____
   _____

10. _____
    _____
    _____

11. _____
    _____
    _____

THEFT AND BURGLARY INVESTIGATION CHECKLIST

1. _____

_____

_____

2. _____

_____

_____

3. _____

_____

_____

4. _____

_____

_____

5. _____

_____

_____

6. _____

_____

_____

7. _____

_____

_____

8. _____

_____

_____

9. _____

_____

_____

10. _____

_____

_____

11. _____

_____

_____

12. _____

_____

_____

13. _____

_____

_____

WARRANT ARREST CHECKLIST

1. _____
   _____
   _____
2. _____
   _____
   _____
3. _____
   _____
   _____

STOLEN VEHICLE REPORT CHECKLISTS

(NO RECOVERY / NO ARREST)

1. _____
   _____
   _____
2. _____
   _____
   _____
3. _____
   _____
   _____
4. _____
   _____
   _____

(RECOVERY / NO ARREST)

1. _____
   _____
   _____
2. _____
   _____
   _____
3. _____
   _____
   _____
4. _____
   _____
   _____

5. _____
_____
_____

6. _____
_____
_____

(RECOVERY / ARREST)

1. _____
_____
_____

2. _____
_____
_____

3. _____
_____
_____

DEATH REPORT INVESTIGATION CHECKLIST

(APPARENT NATURAL / ACCIDENTAL)

1. _____
_____
_____

2. _____
_____
_____

3. _____
_____
_____

4. _____
_____
_____

5. _____
_____
_____

6. _____
_____
_____

7. _____
_____
_____

8. _____
_____
_____

9. _____
_____
_____

10. _____
_____
_____

(APPARENT SUICIDE)

1. _____
_____
_____

2. _____
_____
_____

3. _____
_____
_____

4. _____
_____
_____

ADULT SEXUAL ASSAULT / RAPE INVESTIGATION CHECKLIST

1. _____
_____
_____

2. _____
_____
_____

3. _____
_____
_____

4. _____
_____
_____

5. _____
   _____
   _____

6. _____
   _____
   _____

7. _____
   _____
   _____

8. _____
   _____
   _____

9. _____
   _____
   _____

10. _____
    _____
    _____

CHECKS / CREDIT CARD / FORGERY CASES INVESTIGATION CHECKLIST

(NON-SUFFICIENT FUNDS / CLOSED ACCOUNT CASES)

1. _____
   _____
   _____

2. _____
   _____
   _____

3. _____
   _____
   _____

4. _____
   _____
   _____

5. _____
   _____
   _____

6. _____
   _____
   _____

7. _____
   _____
   _____

8. _____
_____
_____

(FORGERY)

1. _____
_____
_____

2. _____
_____
_____

3. _____
_____
_____

NARCOTICS / UNDER THE INFLUENCE CASES

1. _____
_____
_____

2. _____
_____
_____

3. _____
_____
_____

4. _____
_____
_____

(POSSESSION OF A CONTROLLED SUBSTANCE)

1. _____
_____
_____

2. _____
_____
_____

3. _____
_____
_____

(POSSESSION FOR SALE)

1. _____
   _____
   _____

2. _____
   _____
   _____

3. _____
   _____
   _____

4. _____
   _____
   _____

5. _____
   _____
   _____

6. _____
   _____
   _____

(SALES OR TRANSPORTATION OF A CONTROLLED SUBSTANCE)

1. _____
   _____
   _____

2. _____
   _____
   _____

3. _____
   _____
   _____

4. _____
   _____
   _____

5. _____
   _____
   _____

Guidelines For Writing Practice Reports

1. Utilize an active voice when writing the practice reports, employing past tense when necessary.

2. Use proper language; do not use slang, jargon or police codes unless you explain what it means.

3. Read the entire scenario before you begin to write. Remember to paraphrase unless it is absolutely necessary to quote the person verbatim.

4. Facts may be out of order. It is your responsibility to put the facts in the correct order.

5. Determine what information is necessary and related to the crime; eliminate unnecessary information.

6. Write the report using only the information provided. **Do not add information. The *narrative* is to be based ONLY on the information given on the sheet marked "Practice Report".**

7. You are to write only the narrative. Assume you have already written the first page. It is not necessary to repeat information already provided on the first page (face sheet).

8. There is information missing from just about every report in the following appendix. On a separate piece of paper note what information you think should have been added to the scenario to make your investigation more complete. State the information or the questions that should have been asked to raise the level of the investigation.

9. After you have finished writing your report, critique your work and look for areas that require improvement.

Victim: Robert Wheaton

You are working patrol today.   At 0930 hours you are dispatched to 12349 Sycamore Street, Cypress, regarding a bike that had been stolen from the victim's driveway.   You arrive at 0936 hours. The victim, Robert Wheaton, tells you: "I had my bike parked in my driveway this morning about 8:00 am.   I had just gotten back from an early ride and picked up my morning papers at the 7-11 store just down the street. I didn't lock my bike because I only intended to be inside the house for a couple of minutes. My wife and I started talking and I forgot about the bike being unlocked. Anyway, I guess it was probably about 8:15 a.m. when I came back outside to the driveway and the bike was gone. I didn't see anyone around so I have no idea who might have taken the bike. It's a black Schwinn 10-speed. I don't have the serial number handy but I can probably find it on the receipt. I'll have to check on that and let you know later. I would say the bike was worth about $125.00. Oh, by the way, my USC sport jacket was on the back of the bike, too. It's a male letterman's jacket, size 46, burgundy and gold, with USC on the back. It's worth about $150.00."

He is willing to prosecute.

Narrative:_____

_____

_____

_____

_____

_____

_____

_____

_____

_____

_____

_____

_____

_____

_____

_____

_____

_____

_____

_____

_____

_____

_____

#2.	PRACTICE REPORT	GRAND THEFT

Victim: Joseph Mante

Witness: John McMillan

Date and time crime occurred: Today at 1800 hours

Location crime occurred: 4567 Katella Ave., Cypress, parking lot of Ramada Inn

Date and crime reported to the police: Today at 1815 hours

You are dispatched to take a theft report. You arrive at 1822 hours. The victim says that he parked his pickup truck, a blue, 1991 Dodge Ram Truck (no shell), California license 456 FFH, in the parking lot of the Ramada Inn at 1800 hours. His gardening tools were in the truck bed. The items were locked with a motorcycle chain that was secured with a combination lock.

Items stolen were: a Sears gasoline-powered mower (unknown serial number), valued at $450; a Sears gasoline-powered edger (unknown serial number), valued at $120; a Honda mini-generator, gasoline-powered (unknown serial number), valued at $400.

The victim tells you that he was made aware of the theft by his friend, the witness, who is also the bartender at the Ramada Inn. The witness was in the process of leaving work and saw the suspects tampering with the victim's truck and equipment. The witness ran back inside the bar and told the victim what he saw. The victim ran outside to the parking lot in time to see a truck driving away with his property in the back of it. The truck was a Chevrolet, no shell, dark blue, with tailgate damage (dent). He got only a partial license plate of California 123_ _ _ _. The truck looked to be about 3 to 4 years old. The victim could only see one suspect clearly, the passenger, who looked back at the victim as they drove away. The passenger suspect was described as a Hispanic male about 20 to 24 years old, with dark hair, and wearing a white shirt. The victim cannot describe the passenger's build or height or weight because the suspect was seated in the truck when he saw him. He cannot provide much information on the suspect driver except to say he thought the driver was a male. The victim believes that he could recognize the one suspect and the vehicle, but not the other suspect. The victim is willing to prosecute. He adds that the witness had to leave the scene but would be available later this date for an interview.

Narrative:_____

_____

_____

_____

_____

_____

_____

_____

_____

_____

Victim: Allen Talbot

You are sent to 24909 Mayberry Road, your city, to take a residential burglary report.   You arrive at about 1748 hours. The victim tells you "I locked all the doors and windows to my house this morning when I left for work at about 7:45 a.m. I came home about 5:30 p.m. and found the front door open.   When I went inside, I found that someone had torn my house apart.   The furniture was overturned, drawers were emptied onto the floor, and clothes were removed from the closets. I checked my dresser in the master bedroom and found approximately $300 in cash missing. I see that the scums took my Rolex watch, too. It was on the night table by my bed."

You inspect the house and see that the sliding glass door to the master bedroom has been pried. There are indentations on the metal part of the door near the lock and a screwdriver lies nearby on the patio deck. The rest of the house is a mess. Every room has been ransacked. You check with the nearby neighbors, but no one saw anyone suspicious.   He will prosecute.   You call for a crime scene investigator and Officer Smith arrives to check for fingerprints.   He will write a separate report regarding his findings.

The only thing confirmed stolen besides the cash is the Rolex watch valued at $4,500.00.

Narrative:_____

_____

_____

_____

_____

_____

_____

_____

_____

_____

_____

_____

_____

_____

_____

_____

_____

_____

_____

_____

_____

_____

_____

_____

Victim: Mary Paquin

Witness: Allen Foster

You are dispatched to 1239 S. Dilly Street, your city, to take a vehicle burglary report. You arrive at about 12:22 a.m. The burglary occurred at 11:50 p.m., in the victim's driveway. Entry was through the driver's side window, which was smashed.

The victim tells you that she was awakened just before midnight because her dog, Maxx, was barking. As she started to get up out of bed, she heard glass breaking and ran to the kitchen window, which looks out onto the driveway. The dog continued to bark and she heard footsteps running away from her house, but did not see anyone. Her neighbor, Allen, called her on the phone and told her that he was startled by the same noise of glass breaking. He looked out his kitchen window to see a male running away from the victim's car. The victim called police. She is willing to prosecute.

The witness tells you that he was watching TV in his den when he heard glass breaking. He went to the kitchen window and saw a male exiting the driver's door of his neighbor's car and it looked like the person was holding something. He ran from his house and yelled at the person to stop, but the person ran eastbound on Dilly towards a waiting vehicle and got into that vehicle on the passenger side. He can describe the suspect vehicle only as a compact pick-up truck with a right rear tail light out. It was a dark color pick-up truck and he could not see a license plate or who was driving. The only description he can give of the suspect that he saw was a male of unknown race, with long dark hair past the shoulders, wearing all dark clothing, about 6 feet tall and weighing about 140 pounds. He would not recognize the suspect if he saw him again.

You check the victim's vehicle and see that the driver's side window has been smashed. The compact disk player has been removed from the dash. There are wires hanging down from the dash. There are pliers sitting on the floorboard. The victim says the pliers are not hers. You take the pliers as evidence and book them under tag #29277.

You call for a crime scene investigator, and technician Mitchell, #387, responds to take fingerprints. He will write a separate report. The CD player is an in-dash Kenwood radio combination valued at $500. The serial number is unknown. The victim's vehicle is a 1991 Ford Tempo, 2-door, California license 1FGH987.

Narrative:_____

_____

_____

_____

_____

_____

Victim: Fred Jackson

On today's date at approximately 1010 hours, you are dispatched to a burglary investigation at 1527 E. 103rd St.   When you reach the location, you are met by a black male who identifies himself as Fred Jackson.   Mr. Jackson tells you that he is the owner of Fred's Gun Shop at that address.   He says "I'm tired of getting ripped off.   This is the 3rd time this year I've been robbed. I just installed new locks like you guys told me to do and those creeps still got in."   He says he locked the shop the night before at about 1830 hours.   He returned this morning at 1000 hours to open up.

Fred Jackson says "I unlocked the front door with my key and immediately noticed that the front display counter had been smashed.   That counter is ten feet long and four feet high and two feet wide.   It'll cost me at least $300 to fix the counter case.   There's glass all over.   Those thieving morons took three Colt .45 caliber semi-automatic government model handguns.   I checked all of my other stock and the only other thing missing is a Buck hunting knife.   Those handguns were blue steel, model 1911A1.   The knife has a 4" folding blade and a brown and white bone handle. They were all locked in the case.   The guns are $275.00 each and the knife is $29.50."

You inspect the premises and see that the metal rear door to the business is open 3 inches.   The deadbolt lock is still in the locked position and the door jamb is bent away from the lock itself. You see at the jamb and door edge two pry marks measuring about 1" each.   The victim says that the door will cost $75 to fix.   You take 2 latent fingerprints from the exterior portion of the door. You book the fingerprints into evidence under tag #3456.

Mr. Jackson does not have the serial numbers to the missing guns readily available.   You give him a supplemental property loss sheet and tell him to fill it out and send it to the police department.

After you leave the crime scene, you stop by the only other business, which is located just south of the victim's shop, to talk to any possible witnesses.   The address there is 1525 E. 103rd St., the store is Marv's Fishing Bait and Flies.   A note on the door says the store is closed and Marv is gone fishing and won't be back until next month.

Narrative:_____

_____

_____

_____

_____

_____

_____

_____

_____

Victim: Paul Virt

Witness: Betty Jo Virt

Suspect: Joseph Muldoon

Injuries: Swollen left ankle; refused medical aid

You are called to the victim's residence to take a report of an assault and battery. You arrive at 1500 hours. When you get there, the victim tells you that he was watering his front lawn when the suspect approached him, accusing him of letting his dog defecate on his (the suspect's) front lawn. The victim says that the suspect yelled "Look you - your dog crapped all over my lawn." The victim denied that his dog defecated on his lawn and the suspect went back inside his residence and came back a few minutes later with a broom. The suspect began screaming at him, referring back to the dog defecating on his lawn, and swung at the victim with the broomstick. The victim was able to deflect the broom with his left leg and ankle area, and took the blow on his leg. The victim was struck once only. He then ran into his house and called the police. The suspect ran into his house after the attack. You look at the victim's leg and it is red and starting to swell. The victim does not desire prosecution.

Witness Virt: she is the victim's wife and saw the attack from the kitchen window, about 35 feet from the front lawn. She couldn't hear what they were arguing about but could hear the suspect yelling at her husband and then saw the suspect leave, come back with a broom, and saw the suspect hit her husband's left leg with the broom.

Both the victim and his wife know the suspect as their neighbor and provide you with his name and address.

The suspect says that he did hit the neighbor's leg, believing that the neighbor's dog was responsible for pooping on his lawn. He apologized for the incident and says that he just lost his job and was upset about finding poop on his lawn. He says that the incident will not happen again.

Narrative:_____
_____
_____
_____
_____
_____
_____
_____
_____
_____

#7.	PRACTICE REPORT	DOMESTIC VIOLENCE

Victim: Sally Bowers (wife)

Suspect: Marvin Bowers (husband)

You are working patrol today and are dispatched to a domestic dispute at 1239 Leon Street, Cypress. You arrive at 1945 hours. Your follow-up officer, Smith, #212, arrives at 1946 hours. While you talk with the victim, Officer Smith stands by with the suspect. The victim says: "I called you. I got home from work about ½ hour ago to find my "jerk" husband drinking again. He was in a really rotten mood and I asked him what was wrong and he said that he was fired from work today. I told him that I wasn't surprised because he is always drinking too much. He got really angry at me and when I turned to walk away he grabbed my arm and spun me around. Then he slapped me in the face and it knocked me to the floor. I went into the bathroom and saw that I was starting to get a black right eye. I called you because I'm tired of him beating up on me - this is not the first time, you know, but I'm afraid of him. I don't want him arrested - that'll only make things worse."

The victim refuses your offers of medical care. You see the beginnings of a bruise around the victim's right eye. It is already turning black-and-blue. You take a photograph of the eye. You provide the victim with Domestic Violence form, #209, which provides the victim with information on shelters, counseling, and the right to make an arrest.

You read the Miranda advisement to the suspect and he says "she had no business calling you guys-I told her that I got fired and she started calling me names and a 'drunk'. I never hit her-she hit her face on the door when she stormed out of the room. She's a bitch and she's always bitching about something and calling me names. She can go to hell. I'm going to file for divorce."

You arrest the suspect and charge him with violation of California Penal Code Section 273.5, Spousal Abuse.

Narrative:_____
_____
_____
_____
_____
_____
_____
_____
_____
_____
_____
_____
_____

Victim: Marla Downs

Station Owner and Victim: Steve Due

Reporting Party: Thomas Moody

You are working patrol today and are dispatched to a "211 gas station that just occurred" at 3434 Denni Street. You get the call at 2345 hours and arrive at 2348 hours.   When you arrive, the cashier, Downs, tells you that when the suspect in the robbery was leaving, he put tape on her mouth and tied her hands. The suspect then laid her down in the bathroom which is inside the station. She had been in that position for about 5 minutes when she heard Moody calling out "Anyone here?" She couldn't yell, but she started to kick the bathroom door and Moody came to her rescue. He untied her and took the tape off of her mouth. She then called the police.

Downs continues to tell you that she was working alone this evening at the station as the cashier. She saw a pedestrian, the suspect, approach from the east and come into the station. He walked around for a few minutes looking at the candy bars and magazines. She was on the phone with the station owner about the same time the suspect walked in. When she got off the phone, the suspect turned around and faced her, pointing a gun at her. He said "Give me all the money and fast." She opened the register and started to hand him the bills but he said "Put it in a brown paper bag." She placed the cash in a small brown paper bag. She thinks he got about $100 (all different bills) or less because she had just made a night drop of the day's earlier receipts.

He told her to go into the bathroom (there's only one inside the station). She did so, and he followed her. When she reached the bathroom door, he told her to turn around and to put her hands behind her. She did so, and he tied her wrists with a thick type of twine. When he finished tying her wrists, he put tape over her mouth. She adds that he must have brought the tape and twine with him, because the station has no such items. He then told her to kneel down and when she did, he laid her on her side. He then closed the bathroom door. Within a second or so she heard the glass front door close and a few minutes after that she heard Moody calling to her. She is not injured and doesn't think she would recognize the suspect if she saw him again. She did not hear any cars drive away. Her best estimate of when the crime occurred was 2335 hours. She added that the suspect seemed very calm.

She can't be very specific about the gun the suspect had because she is not very familiar with handguns. She noticed it was chrome, but can't tell you if it was an automatic or revolver or how big it was. She thinks that the suspect may have touched the outside of the bathroom door around the doorknob and also the cashier's counter top.   The suspect did not have any gloves on. She added that she discovered, just prior to your arrival, that the suspect apparently stole her purse, too. She had left it behind the counter on the floor and it is now gone. She describes the purse as a brown leather shoulder bag with strap, value $15.00; contents of the purse were the wallet, with only loose cash, about $20 in miscellaneous bills; brush and comb, value $5; unopened pack of cigarettes, value $3; gold cigarette lighter, value $25.

Moody says he pulled into the gas station to get gas and went into the station to give the cashier his credit card. He waited around for a couple of minutes and no one appeared. He yelled out "Anyone here?" and that's when he heard the victim kicking the bathroom door. He opened the bathroom door, saw that she had been tied up, and freed her. She then called the police. He did not see anyone else in or about the area of the gas station at anytime.

Your observations: you do a walk-through with the victim and she shows you where the twine and tape are still on the bathroom floor where she left them. You collect both and book them under the following tag numbers: twine, #12390; tape, #12391. You go outside and check the parking lot area for any evidence, and find the cashier's purse in a trash can that's behind the gas station. The only item missing from the purse is the cash. You return all the items to Downs. You call for a crime scene investigator and Officer Robin arrives and handles collecting the fingerprints. He will have a supplemental report.

Both victims (the store owner and the clerk) are willing to prosecute. She gives you the description of the suspect: male Caucasian, 20-23 years old, 5'-9", 165 pounds, black hair combed straight back (collar length), unknown color eyes, wearing a white t-shirt, black slacks, unknown shoes, and dark sunglasses.

Narrative:_____

_____
_____
_____
_____
_____
_____
_____
_____
_____
_____
_____
_____
_____
_____
_____
_____
_____
_____
_____
_____
_____
_____

Victim: Lucky Supermarket

Victim: Mary Byers

Witness: Molly Smith

You are working patrol today and are dispatched to Lucky Supermarket at 11390 Salton Sea Drive for a robbery report. You arrive at 0735 hours. You are met by the store manager who is also the victim, Mary Lynn Byers. She tells you the following:

"I got here around 7:30 this morning because we open at 8 and I have to figure the cash drawers before everyone else, the clerks and so forth, get here. The clerks and stock boys get here at 7:30. Well, anyway, I came in the front door like I always do. I locked the doors behind me and I turned off the alarm and nothing looked out of place as far as I could tell. Well, anyway, I walked to the back of the store where the office is, and where the safe is. I heard a noise behind me and I turned around to find a guy with a great big knife pointing it at me and telling me to hurry and open up the safe. In fact I recall exactly what he said. It was 'Hurry up, bitch, and open the safe.' I saw that he was really nervous because he was sweating and shaking the knife like crazy. I opened up the safe and I heard some knocking on the front doors, which I knew had to be a clerk or a stock boy because it was close to 7:30. I handed the cash to him. Anyway, he heard the knock, too, and got really mad and scared and yelled at me asking for the nearest exit. Well, the front doors were still locked, and the back door, which is in the office, was still locked and had a bar over it that was also locked. You can look - the bar is still in place."

"I started to unlock the back door for him, but he grabbed me and started pulling me towards the front doors, all the time holding the knife real close to my throat. He kept saying over and over 'Don't give me a reason to cut your throat, lady. I will, I got nothin to lose.', and that's when I saw Molly standing at the door. She saw him and she started to scream. He yelled at her to shut up and for me to unlock the front doors. I did, and he went running out the doors, southbound on Salton Sea. I didn't see where he went from there. No, I'm not hurt, just scared."

She is confident that she would be able to recognize the suspect and is desirous of prosecution.

The victim also tells you that she has no idea how the suspect entered the store, as he was apparently there when she arrived. She can only give a rough estimate of how much money he got because she'll have to look at the last night's receipts before she can estimate what exactly is missing. She thinks that the amount is approximately $2500 cash (all different bills: 1s, 5s, 10s, and 20s). She tells you the suspect was a male Hispanic, about 20-25 years old, black hair slicked back, about 6' tall, weighing about 145 pounds, wearing a white t-shirt, black Levis jacket, black Levis jeans, and white tennis shoes. The suspect had a very slight limp. The suspect placed the money in the left front pocket of the jacket he was wearing.

Byers takes you on a tour of the store so you can determine how the suspect made entry. You walk into the warehouse located at the rear of the store and find that a roof vent cover has been removed. There are several boxes stacked one on top of each other allowing someone to climb up to or down from the roof vent. The victim says that the vent cover is never off and that it wasn't like that when she closed the store the night before at 11:00 p.m. She says she would have noticed the stacked boxes and the open vent on the walk-through of the building she does every night before she closes, just to make sure that all employees and patrons are out of the store. She adds that she doesn't think the vent is hooked up to the alarm system.

You advise other nearby police cars of the suspect's description. However, they are unable to locate any possible suspects. You call for a crime scene investigator to check for fingerprints on certain surfaces within the store that the suspect may have touched. Officer Brown will handle all the crime scene investigation and collection of evidence, and he will have a separate report.

Next, you talk to witness Molly Smith. She tells you "Well, I tell you the whole sight just scared the poop out of me. I saw this guy holding a knife, a real big knife, at Mary's throat. I didn't know he was inside with her already, because I only saw her car in the parking lot, so I knew she and I were the only ones here. Anyway, I started knocking on the front doors like I always do, and next thing I know she comes to the doors with this guy. I must've started screaming because he started yelling and I saw Mary trying to open the doors with her keys. Once the doors were opened, he pushed past me and I got a real good look at his face. I would know him anywhere."

Witness Smit provides you with this suspect description: male Hispanic, about 25 years old, black hair, 5'-7" to 5'-9" tall, 150-160 pounds, wearing a white T-shirt and black pants.

Description of the store: the store is located in a commercial complex and is a single story building. There are neighboring businesses on each side of the building and an alley that runs behind the store. The alley borders the railroad tracks. The store has one set of double front doors which are locked with a dead bolt lock that requires a key to lock and unlock from the inside or the outside. The rear door has a solid metal horizontal bar which is still in place and is still locked with a combination lock. All doors and windows are hooked up to the alarm which is a burglary alarm only. The alarm is monitored through WestPac Alarms.

Narrative:_____

_____

_____

_____

_____

_____

_____

_____

_____

_____

_____

_____

_____

Victim: Thomas Smythe

Witness #1:   Jonathan Stanley

Witness #2:   Marvin Jaclin

You are dispatched to an assault with a deadly weapon (ADW) investigation at Albertson's food market, 1246 S. Crescent Drive, Huntington Beach. When you get there, you are met by the two witnesses. The victim, Smythe, has a bleeding wound in his upper left thigh and he is lying on the ground. The paramedics are already there and are attending to the victim's injuries. The victim's injuries are not life threatening and the paramedics allow you to question the victim about the circumstances of his injury. You can see the wound and it appears to be a bullet wound.

The victim tells you that he and his roommate, Witness #1, Stanley, were at the market doing their weekly grocery shopping. Once inside the store, the victim realized he had left his wallet in the glove compartment of his car. The victim returned to his car leaving the witness inside the store, shopping. When the victim got to his car, he saw an unknown male Mexican adult inside the car. It appeared that the person was trying to start the car. The victim walked up to his car and yelled at the suspect to get out of his car. The suspect bolted out of the driver's door and the victim tried to grab onto him to stop him. The two of them fell to the ground, punching each other. Suddenly and without any warning, the suspect pulled a gun out from the jacket he was wearing, pointed it at the victim, and fired the gun, hitting the victim in the thigh. The suspect fled on foot westbound through the parking lot and onto westbound Ward Street. The victim said that this occurred about 10 minutes prior to your arrival.

You immediately announce a broadcast of the suspect's description for nearby police units. The victim describes the suspect as a male Hispanic, about 22-25 years old, 5'-9" tall, 165-175 pounds, unknown color eyes, black hair, wearing a white T-shirt, brown leather aviator jacket, blue jeans, and unknown shoes. The victim can describe the gun as a chrome revolver, possibly a 4 inch revolver. The victim would recognize the suspect if he saw him again and will prosecute.

Witness Stanley said that he was wondering what was taking the victim so long just to get his wallet. As the witness walked outside, he heard the shot and saw his roommate fall to the ground. He did not see the victim and suspect struggling on the ground. He ran to the victim and saw the suspect run westbound from the area and westbound on Ward St. He could only describe the gun as a chrome revolver. The witness said that he believed the suspect description given by the victim was correct but he added that he thought the suspect had been wearing a baseball hat that was green with white unknown lettering on the front of the hat. He says he would be able to recognize the suspect if he saw him again.

Witness #2, Jaclin, said he was in the parking lot loading up his truck when he saw the suspect and the victim struggling on the ground. The witness started to run to the victim's aid and heard the shot. He saw the suspect run westbound on Ward Street. The witness agrees with the description of the suspect that was provided, except he can't recall the clothing the suspect was wearing. He confirms the suspect was male, Hispanic, about 20-25 years old, between 5'7" and 5'10" tall, weight between 150-175 pounds, black hair, and unknown eye color.

Paramedic Winchell, #346, tells you that the victim's injury is a through-and-through gunshot wound of the thigh which will require additional medical attention. Medix ambulance will transport the victim to Huntington Beach Memorial Hospital at 12398 Lakeshore Drive, Huntington Beach.

Before you leave the scene you inspect the victim's vehicle. You see it is parked on the east side of the market. It is a 1993 Cadillac El Dorado ITS, License CBASIC, all black, and is registered to the victim. You see that the driver's window is broken out and the ignition has been pulled from the steering column. There is a screwdriver on the floor of the car near the accelerator pedal. You can't find the victim's wallet in the glove compartment. The glove compartment door is open.

Before the victim is taken to the hospital, you ask him about the screwdriver. He says that the screwdriver is not his. He also tells you the car was locked up, the windows were rolled up and the vehicle was in perfect order when he parked it. You request a crime scene investigator to take photos of the vehicle and to collect all evidence.

Narrative:_____

_____

_____

_____

_____

_____

_____

_____

_____

_____

_____

_____

_____

_____

_____

_____

_____

_____

_____

_____

_____

_____

_____

Victim: Marion David

Reporting party: Ken Mathis

You are working patrol today and are dispatched to 10933 South Street regarding an attempted suicide. Dispatch tells you that the person who attempted suicide is Marion David, who supposedly lives at the address. The reporting party is a hot-line volunteer, Ken Mathis, of United Churches Suicide Hot Line, located at 278 N. Wilshire, Anaheim. Mathis tells your dispatcher that David had called the hot line and had told the volunteer that she was planning on killing herself with sleeping pills. Mathis kept David on the phone long enough to trace the call through the telephone company and discovered that David was calling from an address in your city.

You arrive at 0930 hours and the follow-up officer, Officer S. Parker, #3645, arrives at 0931 hours. You knock on the front door of the residence and David comes to the door and lets you in. She tells you she is extremely depressed and has been talking to a hot-line. The phone is still off the hook and Mathis is still on the line. While Officer Parker sits with David, you talk to Mathis, who confirms all the information already provided to you.

David tells you that she is depressed because of her father dying in a boating accident two days ago in San Francisco. Her father was her only living relative and now she claims to have no one else locally who cares about her. She says her old boyfriend, Sam Horner, and she broke up about two months ago when she caught him fooling around with an old girlfriend. David says that for the last two years she has been seeing a psychiatrist for depression and has been taking two medications. Her doctor is Dr. Jerry Bump, phone # 310-388-9990. She admits to taking all the pills in the two medication bottles. You check the containers left on the counter in the kitchen and both are empty. One bottle is marked Valium and the other is marked Paxil.

You request paramedics, who arrive and treat the victim at the scene for ingestion of the pills. The victim has now become incoherent, possibly due to the medication. She is mumbling and cannot tell you anything else. The paramedics transport David to the hospital, Charter Hospital, 2233 N. Lemon St., for further treatment. The attending physician is Dr. Jake Halls. He pumps her stomach and tells you that due to the circumstances of the attempt suicide he will admit her to the hospital for mental evaluation by the hospital's psychiatric staff. You complete the Welfare and Institutions Code Section 5150[4] form which states that the victim is a danger to herself. You leave her in the custody of the doctor.

[4]California Welfare and Institutions Code Section 5150 states, in pertinent part: "**5150. When any person, as a result of mental disorder, is a danger to others, or to himself or herself, or gravely disabled, a peace officer, member of the attending staff, as defined by regulation, of an evaluation facility designated by the county, designated members of a mobile crisis team provided by Section 5651.7, or other professional person designated by the county may, upon probable cause, take, or cause to be taken, the person into custody and place him or her in a facility designated by the county and approved by the State Department of Mental Health as a facility for 72-hour treatment and evaluation.**"

Narrative:_____

_____

_____

_____

_____

_____

_____

_____

_____

_____

_____

_____

_____

_____

_____

_____

_____

_____

_____

_____

_____

_____

_____

_____

_____

_____

_____

_____

_____

_____

_____

_____

_____

_____

Victim: Daryl Bothom

Witness: David Ramsey

Today at 0735 hours while working patrol, you are dispatched to a possible suicide at 12234 Matson Drive, La Palma. You arrive at 0740 hours and meet the witness, Ramsey, who is waiting for you as you drive up. He tells you that the victim is inside the house. Officer Smith, #234, arrives as your backup officer and the two of you quickly check the residence for any other people; there are none and you secure the residence. You quickly check for signs of life in the victim and find none. The paramedics arrive at about the same time you do.

Ramsey says he has known the victim for about 5 years. They are next-door neighbors. Ramsey had gone to the victim's residence at 7:30 a.m. The two had made arrangements to go golfing today and they were supposed to meet at 7:15 a.m. Ramsey telephoned the victim at about 7:15 a.m., and when he didn't answer, he went next door. When he knocked on the victim's front door there was no answer. He tried the door knob and the door was unlocked. He walked into the living room and found the victim on the floor. He looked dead. He saw that the victim had a bloody head and saw the gun near the victim. He used the phone in the kitchen to call the police. He touched nothing else in the residence or on the body.

Ramsey says he talked to Bothom the night before at about 1800 hours. They confirmed their golf date. Ramsey says that he lives next door and heard nothing unusual all night and saw no one at the residence other than the victim. Ramsey has no knowledge of anyone else living at the residence with the victim. He knows of no reason why the victim would kill himself, other than the fact that he had been out of work for about 8 months. Ramsey does not know of any relatives, girlfriend, etc.

Station 21, Orange County Fire Department, Engine #16, Paramedics John Dixon, #23, and Mark De Gaulle, #298, respond. They pronounce the victim dead at 0744 hours. At 0744 hours you call for a deputy coroner.

You see what appears to be the beginning of rigor mortis on the body. Blood has coagulated on the victim's left temple and on the floor. You see what appear to be deposits of black powder on the temple, surrounding the entry wound. The victim is lying on his back with his head facing northeast. There is a handgun in the victim's left hand and his index finger is still surrounding the trigger. There are splatters of blood on the handgun. The victim is fully clothed in a pair of blue Levi's, tennis shoes and socks and a white T-shirt. The T-shirt has blood on it. You don't see any injuries on the body except for the head wound.

On a nearby coffee table you see a box of .38 caliber ammunition. The box is open. You also see a leather handgun carrying case on the table. The residence is a single story house, with three bedrooms, a kitchen, and two bathrooms; there is an unattached garage. You check the house and all the doors and windows appear to be intact. A rear door and all windows are still locked. The residence is tidy and appears to be clean. Nothing is out of order. You do not find a suicide note.

A vehicle, a red 1987 Ford Thunderbird, license 897GGH, is in the garage. It is registered to the victim. It is neat and tidy.

You ask the dispatcher to check the gun through the Department of Justice records and are told the handgun in the victim's hand is registered to him. It is a Smith and Wesson revolver, Model 36, .38 caliber, serial #98246 and was registered at the time of purchase on January 10, 1987.

The Coroner's Investigator is Sam More, #235, and he arrives at 0930 hours. Investigator More, after checking the condition of the body, estimates the time of death to be within the past 10-12 hours. More adds that the death appears to be due to a self-inflicted gunshot wound. You relay the information Ramsey provided when he found the body.

Investigator More inventories the body and finds a wallet in the victim's left rear pants pocket. The wallet contains the victim's driver's license, one $5 bill, a Shell credit card, and miscellaneous photographs. A Timex watch and a silver ring were also removed from the body. These personal items are bagged and inventoried by the coroner. The coroner keeps them and gives you a copy of the inventory sheet.

Investigator More removes the gun from the victim's hand and confirms the serial number with you. The gun, ammunition box, and all ammunition are also taken by the coroner. The coroner's office has the body removed at 1130 hours. More tells you that they will attempt to locate the relatives and will notify them of the death.

Narrative:_____

_____
_____
_____
_____
_____
_____
_____
_____
_____
_____
_____
_____
_____
_____
_____
_____
_____
_____
_____

#13. PRACTICE REPORT - DRUNK IN PUBLIC ARREST

Arrestee: Jay Jodel

On today's date and time you are on patrol in a marked police car in the general vicinity of Ball Road and Walker Street. You see Jodel walking westbound. You see that he seems to be having difficulty walking because you see him stumble and almost fall, twice. You stop to check on his welfare, thinking that he is either ill or drunk. You park your car at the west curb and stop him. You smell a strong odor of alcohol, and he admits to you that he has been drinking some beers at the local bar, the Fuzzy Bear Saloon. You are familiar with the bar, which is about 3 blocks away. When he speaks to you, he mumbles and you can barely understand what he is saying. When you ask him what time it is, he tells you that it's 5:00 a.m., even though it's really 12:00 noon. You can see that his eyes are bloodshot and watery. His face is red and flushed. His clothing is in poor condition, as it is dirty and it looks like he urinated in his pants. You see what appears to be vomit on the front of his shirt. You ask him for his driver's license and it states that he lives in Montebello. He admits that he has no idea how he got to your city. You conclude that he is intoxicated and is unable to care for himself, a violation of California Penal Code Section 647(f), drunk in public, and you arrest him. You drive him to the Anaheim Police Department for booking and detention. He is held for 4 hours and then released.

Narrative:_____

_____

_____

_____

_____

_____

_____

_____

_____

_____

_____

_____

_____

_____

_____

_____

_____

_____

_____

_____

_____

Victim: Ralph's Food Market
Witness #1:   James Lipton
Witness #2:   Larry Earle
Suspect: Jerry Evans

You are working patrol today and are dispatched to a "shoplifter in custody" at Ralph's Food Market, 1203 West Street, Cypress. You arrive at 1930 hours. When you arrive you speak to the manager, who is witness #1, James Lipton. He takes you to his office where the suspect is being detained by another store employee, witness #2, Larry Earle. The suspect identifies himself as Jerry Evans.

Lipton tells you "I was watching the floor from my TV monitors here in my office. I can see the entire store from here and if I see something suspicious, I let Larry know by radio and then he also keeps an eye on the person. Well, anyway, I saw this guy (he points to the suspect) walking around the store for about half an hour. This all happened about 45 minutes ago. Anyway, I noticed him because he just kept wandering around and didn't seem to be picking up anything to buy. In fact, I had Larry go up to him to see if he needed some help finding something, but he said he didn't. When Larry left the aisle the guy was in, I kept watching the guy on the monitor and saw him pick up two bottles of wine from the liquor department. I couldn't tell what kind of wine it was. He put the two bottles under his shirt and walked out of the store, never stopping to pay for the two items. I had Larry follow him outside to the front sidewalk, where I caught up to them and grabbed the guy's shirt. He dropped both bottles and they broke. The pieces of glass are still on the sidewalk. They were two bottles of Blue Nun wine and they cost $5.99. I already told him he was under arrest for theft."

You talk to Earle and he says "I was working the floor when my boss, Jim, called me on the radio and said to watch this guy (he points to the suspect). I went up to him and asked him if he needed help. He said no. He was in the dairy products section then. I walked away and about 1 minute later my boss radioed me again that the guy had just stolen 2 bottles of wine. I saw him as he walked by at least two or three open cash registers and didn't stop to pay. I kept following him, and when we were out in front of the store, my boss caught up to us and grabbed the guy by the arm. That's when the bottles fell and broke. We brought him back here and I called you guys."

Lipton signs the private person's arrest form and tells the suspect that he has arrested him for theft. You take custody of the suspect and handcuff him. You Mirandize him but he refuses to make any statements other than to provide you his name, etc. You search him and he has $9 in cash on him. He has no credit cards or checks on him. On the way out of the store you see the broken wine bottles. You transport him to jail for booking on the charge of petty theft, California Penal Code Section 488. He is then released on a citation, number CY348769.

Narrative:_____

_____

_____

_____

_____

_____

_____

_____

_____

_____

_____

_____

_____

_____

_____

_____

_____

_____

_____

_____

_____

_____

_____

_____

_____

_____

_____

_____

_____

_____

_____

_____

_____

_____

_____

_____

_____

_____

_____

_____

_____

_____

_____

_____

_____

_____

15.PRACTICE REPORT - ARREST FOR POSSESSION OF A CONTROLLED SUBSTANCE AND A CONCEALED WEAPON

Arrestee: Cassione

You are working patrol today in a marked patrol car. You are driving southbound on Main Street, approaching 15th Street, when you see Cassione standing on the northwest corner. When you get closer, you see what appears to be a clear plastic bag in the suspect's right hand. This area is known for a high number of narcotic arrests. The suspect looks at you, quickly drops the bag on the sidewalk, and walks eastbound on 15th Street.

You immediately park your unit, get out, and pick up the bag. It is a small zip-lock sandwich bag, about 4" by 4". It contains a white powdery substance resembling cocaine. You call for another officer and you start to drive after the suspect. You catch up to the suspect at the southwest corner of 14th Street and Main. You arrest him for violation of Health and Safety Code Section 11350, Possession of a Controlled Substance. Your backup is Officer J. Start, #3480, and he stands by while you make the arrest and handcuff the suspect. You search the suspect and find a concealed .357 magnum, Smith and Wesson handgun in his right waistband. You charge him with violation of California Penal Code Section 12025, Possession of a Concealed Weapon. You check him for signs of being under the influence, but he isn't. You read him his Miranda rights, but he refuses to tell you anything. He makes no statements regarding the crime. You handcuff him, place him in the back seat of your patrol car, and drive him to the police station.

The weapon is a stainless steel revolver with wooden grips and a 6" barrel. It's a Model 66 and the serial number is F14722. The ammunition, 6 bullets, is removed from the gun and is booked with the gun under the same evidence tag # of 12390. The contraband in the baggie is Valtox- tested **(in-the-field chemical test used by many law enforcement agencies to identify many commonly seized drugs such as cocaine, hashish, amphetamines, marijuana, methamphetamines, etc.)** and proves to be cocaine, weighing approximately 2 ounces. The cocaine is booked under evidence tag #12391.

Narrative:_____

_____

_____

_____

_____

_____

_____

_____

_____

_____

_____

_____

Arrestee: John J. Doe

On today's date you are working patrol in a marked police car. During briefing you are told by Detective R. Holt, #3489, that a felony arrest warrant, #A120987, has been issued for John J. Doe, a male Caucasian, blond hair and brown eyes, 6'-1", 170 pounds, DOB 1-23-61. He is wanted for violation of California Penal Code Section 211, robbery. The robbery occurred on 4-15-97 at Sunflower Liquors, 1880 W. Temple Street, Anaheim, case #9201290. The suspect used a .38 caliber 2" chrome revolver in the robbery. He was seen driving away from the location in a white-over-blue 2-door Chevrolet Monte Carlo, license ABC 123. The car is registered to Jane Simple of 212 N. Bendon Way, your city. You check your department's field interrogation (FI) file and find a recent FI on Jane Simple, listing her current address as 3489 W. 3rd St., Anaheim, California.

Since Jane Simple lives in your patrol area, you and your partner, Officer Jeff Morton, #3784, decide to check her address to see if suspect John J. Doe is there. You and your partner drive to Jane Simple's residence; you see the car used in the robbery parked in the driveway of her residence. You draw your handgun. You see a person matching the description of the robbery suspect run from the front yard towards the backyard. He looks directly at you and your partner and you yell "Stop! Police!" He stops. You ask him his name and he tells you that it's John J. Doe. After you confirm the suspect's name and physical description, you advise the suspect that he is under arrest for California Penal Code Section 211, Robbery, and tell him about the warrant. Officer Morton stands by while you search the suspect.   You find a Smith and Wesson .38 caliber, 2" chrome revolver in his rear right pocket. It is fully loaded. You remove the gun from the suspect and unload it. You do not question the suspect nor do you advise him of his Miranda rights.

_____
_____
_____
_____
_____
_____
_____
_____
_____
_____
_____
_____
_____
_____

Complete the following reports and attempt to answer questions that are not addressed. After you have completed the report, compare your discovery with the "missing information checklist" that follows the report.

REPORT #1: ASSAULT AND BATTERY	

☐ Follow-up Investigation   DR#:
06-001
☐ Supplemental Report   Page
2 of 2
■ Narrative of Incident

INJURY

Swollen left ankle of victim Virt

On the previously listed date and time I was dispatched to the listed address regarding an assault and battery. I arrived at 1500 hours. The victim, Virt, said he was watering his front lawn when the suspect, his neighbor, Muldoon, approached him. Muldoon yelled at Virt "look you - your dog crapped all over my lawn." Virt denied that his dog had defecated on Muldoon's lawn. Muldoon went back into his residence and returned a few minutes later with a broom. Muldoon started yelling at Virt again, referring back to the dog defecating on Muldoon's lawn. While yelling he swung the broom at Virt. Virt was able to deflect the broom with his left leg and ankle area, and took the blow on his leg. Virt was struck once only. Virt ran into his house and called police. Muldoon ran into his house after the attack.

I looked at Virt's leg and saw that it was red and starting to swell. Virt does not desire prosecution. The only witness to the attack was the victim's wife, Betty Virt. She said she had been at the kitchen window, about 35 feet from the front lawn. She couldn't hear what they were arguing about but could hear Muldoon yelling at her husband. She saw the suspect leave and return with a broom. She saw the suspect hit her husband's left leg with the broom.

Both the victim and his wife know the suspect as their neighbor and gave me his name and address.

Muldoon said he believed that Virt's dog had defecated on his lawn and he admitted to the attack. Muldoon apologized for the incident and explained that he had just lost his job and was upset about finding feces on his lawn. Muldoon said he would not repeat the incident.

REPORT #2: DOMESTIC VIOLENCE

☐ Follow-up Investigation   DR#: 06-002

INJURY

Bruised right eye of victim Bowers (photo attached)

On the previously listed date and time I was dispatched to the listed address regarding a domestic dispute. I arrived at 1945 hours. The follow-up officer, Smith, #212, arrived at 1946 hours. While I talked to the victim, Officer Smith stood-by with the suspect.

The victim, Sally Bowers, said she had arrived home at about 1915 hours and found that her husband, the suspect, Marvin Bowers, had been drinking. He was in a bad mood and when she asked him what was wrong he told her he had been fired from his job. Sally said she wasn't surprised because he drinks too much. He got angry at her and when she turned to walk away he grabbed her arm and spun her around. He slapped her on the face knocking her to the floor. She went into the bathroom and saw bruising beginning to form creating a black right eye. She said "I called you because I'm tired of him beating up on me - this is not the first time, you know, but I'm afraid of him. I don't want him arrested - that'll only make things worse."

The victim refused any medical aid. I could see the start of a black and blue right eye. I took a photo of the eye. I gave the victim the Domestic Violence form, #209, which provided the victim with information on shelters, counseling, and the right to make an arrest.

I read the Miranda advisement to the suspect and he said "She had no business calling you guys- I told her I was fired and she started calling me names and a 'drunk'.   I never hit her- she hit her face on the door when she stormed out of the room. She's a bitch and she's always bitching about something and calling me names. She can go to hell; I'm going to file for divorce."

I arrested the suspect and charged him with violation of California Penal Code Section 273.5, Spousal Abuse.

_____

_____

_____

_____

_____

_____

_____

_____

_____

_____

_____

REPORT #3: ROBBERY

PROPERTY LOSS

$100 Cash   U.S. currency; miscellaneous bills (victim #1/Due) $100.00

$ 25 Cash   U.S. currency, miscellaneous bills (victim #2/Downs) $ 25.00

1 - leather handbag and contents: brush, comb, pack of cigarettes, gold cigarette lighter (recovered and returned to victim #2/Downs)

Total Combined Loss $125.00

EVIDENCE

1 - Twine   Tag # 12390

1 - Tape   Tag # 12391

She said she was not injured. She thought the crime occurred about 10 minutes before she called the police. She did not hear any cars drive from the area. She didn't think that she would be able to recognize the suspect if she saw him again. She provided the description of the suspect that appears on page 1 of this report. She said the suspect seemed very calm.

She could not provide much information about the suspect's gun because she is not familiar with handguns. She saw that the gun was chrome but didn't know if it was a revolver or semi-automatic or how big it was. She thought the suspect may have touched the outside of the bathroom door around the doorknob and also the cashier's counter top. The suspect did not wear gloves.

She said that just before I arrived, she discovered that her purse had been stolen. She had left the purse behind the counter on the floor, and now the purse was gone.

The Reporting Party, Moody, said he drove into the gas station to get gas and went into the station to give the cashier his credit card. He waited for a couple of minutes and no one appeared. He yelled out "anyone here?" and that was when he heard the victim kicking the bathroom door. He opened the bathroom door, saw that she had been tied up, and freed her. He did not see anyone else in or around the area of the gas station at anytime.

I walked through the business with Downs and she showed me where the tape and twine had been left on the bathroom floor. I collected both the twine and tape and later booked them into evidence. I walked outside to look for evidence, and while looking through a trash can I found the victim's purse. After she verified that all the contents except the cash were still there, the purse and contents were returned to her.

I requested a crime scene investigator and Officer Robin arrived to handle collecting fingerprints. He will have a supplemental report.

Both the victims are willing to prosecute.

REPORT #4:   ROBBERY, BURGLARY, AND ASSAULT WITH A DEADLY WEAPON

PROPERTY LOSS
$2,500 cash, U.S. currency, miscellaneous bills $2,500.00

On the previously listed date and time I was dispatched to the listed address, Lucky Supermarket, regarding a robbery report. I arrived at 0735 hours. The victim, Byers, told me she is the manager of the store. She arrived this morning at about 0730 hours. The store opens at 0800 hours. Other employees also usually start to arrive at 0730. She entered through the front doors. She locked the doors behind her and turned off the alarm. She said that she noticed nothing out of place. She walked to the back of the store where her office is and where the safe is located. She heard a noise behind her and when she turned around she saw the suspect holding a knife and pointing it at her. He told her to hurry and open up the safe. She recalled exactly what the suspect said. It was "Hurry up, bitch, and open the safe." She said the suspect seemed very nervous because he was sweating and the hand holding the knife was shaking. While she was opening the safe she heard someone knocking on the front doors, and she knew it had to be an employee. She handed the cash to the suspect and he put it in his left front jacket pocket. The suspect had also heard the knocking and yelled at her to find another way for him to get out.

The store is located in a commercial complex and is a single story building. There are neighboring businesses on each side of the building and an alley that runs behind the store. The alley borders the railroad tracks. The store has one set of double front doors that are locked with a dead bolt lock. The deadbolt requires a key to lock and unlock from the inside or the outside. I saw that the rear door still had a horizontal bar in place and it was locked with a combination lock. All the doors and windows are connected to the alarm, which is a burglar alarm only. The alarm is monitored through WestPac Alarms.

The back office door was still locked, with a bar in place, so she started to unlock it so he could get out that way. But as she was doing that, he grabbed her and started pulling her towards the front door, all the time holding the knife close to her throat. He kept saying to her, over and over, "Don't give me a reason to cut your throat, lady. I will, I got nothin to lose." She saw the witness, Smit, standing at the door. Smit saw the suspect and she started to scream. The suspect yelled at her to 'shut up' and told Byers to unlock the front doors. She did, and the suspect ran southbound on Salton Sea. She did not see where he ran from there. Byers said that she was scared but unhurt. She is confident that she would be able to recognize the suspect and wants to prosecute.

Byers said that she had no idea how the suspect entered the store, because he was already there when she entered. She could only estimate the monetary loss at the time of this report. She said by examining the previous night's receipts she could better estimate the loss. She gave the description of the suspect appears on page 1 of this report. She added that the suspect had a slight limp.

I broadcasted the suspect's description that the weapon was a knife, the estimated loss, and the suspect's direction of travel to nearby police officers but they were unable to locate any probable suspect.

The witness, Smit, said that she didn't know anyone else was in the store with Byers because she only saw Byers' car in the parking lot. When Smit got to the front doors and knocked, she saw the suspect holding a knife at Byers' throat. Smit thought that she probably started to scream, at which point the suspect started to yell and Byers tried to open the front doors with her keys. Once Byers opened the doors, the suspect pushed past Smit. Smit said "I got a real good look at his face. I would know him anywhere." Smit described the suspect as a male Hispanic, about 25 years old, black hair, 5'-7" to 5'-9" tall, 150-160 pounds, wearing a white t-shirt and black pants.

Byers escorted me on a tour of the building so I could determine how the suspect got into the store. We walked into the warehouse located at the rear of the store. I saw that a roof vent cover had been removed. I saw several boxes stacked on top of one another, which would allow someone to climb up to or down from the roof vent. Byers said the vent cover is never off and that it wasn't like that when she closed the store the night before at 2300 hours. She said that every night before she leaves she takes a tour of the building just to make sure that all employees and patrons are gone. She said she would've noticed the stacked boxes and removed vent cover. She didn't believe the vent was connected to the alarm system.

I called for a crime scene investigator and Officer Brown arrived to handle the collection of evidence. He will write a separate report.

_____
_____
_____
_____
_____
_____
_____
_____
_____
_____
_____
_____
_____
_____
_____
_____
_____
_____
_____
_____
_____
_____
_____
_____
_____
_____

REPORT #5: ROBBERY;ASSAULT, DEADLY WEAPON

<u>INJURIES</u>

One gunshot wound in victim's upper left thigh

On the previously listed date and time, I was dispatched to an assault with a deadly weapon investigation at Albertson's Food Market at the listed address. When I arrived, I was met by both witnesses. The victim, Smythe, was lying down. I saw that his upper left thigh was bleeding from what appeared to be a gunshot wound. The paramedics told me the victim's injury was not life-threatening, so they allowed me to talk to him.

The victim said that he and his roommate, witness #1, Stanley, were at the market doing their weekly grocery shopping. After they were inside the store, Smythe realized that he had left his wallet in the glove compartment of his car. Smythe returned to his car and Stanley stayed inside the store to shop. When Smythe reached his car, he saw the suspect inside it. It appeared that the suspect was trying to start the car. Smythe walked up to his car and yelled at the suspect to get out of his car. The suspect jumped out of the car from the driver's side; Smythe tried to grab onto him to stop him. The two of them fell to the ground, punching each other. Suddenly, and without any warning, the suspect pulled a gun out from a pocket of the jacket he was wearing, pointed the gun at Smythe and fired it. The bullet hit Smythe in the thigh. Smythe said the suspect fled on foot westbound through the parking lot and then westbound onto Ward Street.

Smythe gave the description of the suspect that appears on page 1 of this report. He described the suspect's gun as a chrome revolver, possibly a "4-inch" revolver. Smythe said that he would recognize the suspect if he saw him again and will prosecute. I broadcasted the suspect's description, weapon and direction of travel to other nearby police units.

Witness #1, Stanley, said he was wondering what was taking Smythe so long just to get his wallet. As Stanley walked outside, he heard a shot and saw Smythe on the ground. Stanley did not see the suspect and Smythe struggling on the ground. As Stanley ran toward Smythe, he saw the suspect run westbound on Ward St. Stanley said he would be able to recognize the suspect if he saw him again. Stanley could only describe the suspect's gun as a chrome revolver. Stanley said the description provided by Smythe was correct, but he added that he thought the suspect had been wearing a green baseball hat with white unknown lettering on the front of the hat.

Witness #2, Jaclin, said he was in the parking lot loading up his truck when he saw the suspect and Smythe struggling on the ground. Jaclin started to run to Smythe's aid and heard the shot. He saw the suspect run away, westbound on Ward Street. He said the suspect was a male Hispanic, about 20-25 years old, 5' 7" to 5'10", about 150-175 pounds, black hair and unknown eye color.

I inspected Smythe's vehicle, which was parked on the east side of the market. The vehicle, an all black 1993 Cadillac El Dorado STS, license plate CLASIC, is registered to Smythe. I saw that the driver's window was broken out and the ignition had been pulled from the steering column. I saw a screwdriver on the floor of the car near the accelerator pedal. I saw the glove compartment was open and I looked for Smythe's wallet, but it was not there.

Paramedic Winchell, #346, said the victim had a through-and-through gunshot wound of the thigh and would require additional medical attention. Before the ambulance took Smythe to the hospital, I asked him if the screwdriver was his and he said it wasn't. Smythe said the car had been locked and all of the windows had been rolled up. Medix ambulance took Smythe to Huntington Beach Memorial Hospital at 12398 Lakeshore Drive, Huntington Beach.

I requested a crime scene investigator to take photos of the vehicle and to collect all evidence.

_____
_____
_____
_____
_____
_____
_____
_____
_____
_____
_____
_____
_____
_____
_____
_____
_____
_____
_____
_____
_____
_____
_____
_____
_____
_____

REPORT #6: ATTEMPTED SUICIDE

On the previously listed date and time, I was dispatched to the listed address regarding an attempted suicide. While en route, dispatch said the reporting party was a hot-line volunteer, Ken Mathis, of United Churches Suicide Hot Line in Anaheim. Mathis told dispatch that David called the hotline and told him that she was going to kill herself with sleeping pills. Mathis kept David on the line long enough for the call to be traced to the address that dispatch had sent me to.

I arrived at 0930 hours and my follow-up officer, Officer S. Parker, #3645, arrived at about 0931 hours. We knocked on the front door of the residence and David came to the door and let us in. She said she was extremely depressed and she had been talking with someone on suicide hot-line. The phone was still off the hook and Mathis was still on the line. While Officer Parker stayed with David, I talked to Mathis, who confirmed the information that dispatch had previously given me.

David told me she was depressed because her father had died in a boating accident two days ago in San Francisco. She said her father had been her only living relative and she had no one locally who cared about her. Her old boyfriend, Sam Horner, and she had broken up about two months ago when she caught him with an old girlfriend. David said she had been seeing a psychiatrist for depression and had been taking two medications. Her doctor is Dr. Jerry Bump, phone # 310-388-9990. She admitted to swallowing all the pills from the two medication bottles. I looked at the bottles left on the counter in the kitchen and both were empty. One bottle was marked 'Valium' and the other was marked 'Paxil.'

I requested that paramedics be sent. Once they arrived, they treated David for ingestion of the pills. David had now become incoherent, possibly as a result of medication. She started to mumble and could not tell me anything else.

The paramedics took David to Charter Hospital, 2233 N. Lemon St., for further treatment. Dr. Jake Hall pumped her stomach. He said that due to the circumstances, he would admit her to the hospital for mental evaluation by the hospital's psychiatric staff.

I completed the Welfare and Institutions Code Section 5150 form stating that I considered David a danger to herself, and left her in the custody of Dr. Hall.

_____

_____

_____

_____

_____

_____

_____

_____

_____

_____

_____

_____

REPORT #7:   SUICIDE

On the previously listed date and time, I was dispatched to the listed address to investigate a possible suicide. When the paramedics and I arrived at 0740 hours, we saw the witness, Ramsey, standing outside the victim's residence. Ramsey pointed to the house and said the victim, Bothom, was inside. Officer Smith, #234, and I checked the residence for any other people; there were none. We secured the residence. I looked at Bothom and saw a bloody wound in his left temple. I also saw a handgun in his left hand. I checked Bothom for signs of life and found none. Orange County Fire Department, Engine #16, Station 21, Paramedics J. Dixon, #23, and M. De Gaulle, #298, pronounced Bothom dead at 0744 hours. At 0744 hours, I requested a deputy coroner be sent to the scene.

Ramsey said that he had known Bothom, his next-door neighbor, for about 5 years. The two of them had made arrangements to go golfing today. Ramsey said he telephoned Bothom at about 0715 hours and when he didn't answer he went next door.   When he knocked on the victim's front door, there was no answer.   He tried the doorknob; the door was unlocked. He walked into the living room and found Bothom on the floor. Ramsey said that when he saw Bothom's bloody head and the gun in Bothom's hand, he thought Bothom was dead. Ramsey said that he touched nothing and called the police from Bothom's kitchen phone.

Ramsey said he and Bothom had talked the night before at about 1800 hours. They confirmed their golf date. Ramsey said he lives next door, that he heard nothing unusual all night, and that he hadn't seen anyone at the residence other than the victim.   Ramsey had no knowledge of anyone else living at the residence with the victim. Ramsey could not explain why Bothom would kill himself. He did say that Bothom had been out of work for about 8 months. Ramsey does not know if Bothom had any relatives, a girlfriend, etc.

While waiting for the deputy coroner to arrive, I saw that Bothom's body was beginning to stiffen and blood had coagulated on his left temple and on the floor.   I saw what appeared to be deposits of black powder on the temple, surrounding the entry wound.   Bothom was lying on his back, with his head facing northeast.   The handgun was still in Bothom's left hand and his finger was still around the trigger. I saw splatters of blood on the handgun. The victim was fully clothed in a pair of blue Levi's, a white T-shirt, tennis shoes, and socks. I saw blood on the T-shirt. I saw no injuries to the body other than the head wound.

I saw, on a nearby coffee table, an opened box of .38 caliber ammunition.   Next to it was a leather handgun carrying case.

I checked the house and it was tidy and clean. Nothing appeared out of order. I could not find a suicide note. The house is single story, with three bedrooms, a kitchen, and two bathrooms; there is an unattached garage.   A vehicle, a red 1987 Ford Thunderbird, license 897GGH, was parked in the garage. It is registered to Bothom. The car was neat and tidy.

Deputy Coroner S. More, Badge #235, arrived at 0930 hours. I told him what Ramsey had told me as to how he found the body. More estimated the time of death to be within the past 10-16 hours and added that the injury appeared to be a self-inflicted gunshot wound.

More removed the gun from Bothom's hand and confirmed the serial number.   Upon checking with the Department of Justice records, I learned the gun was registered to Bothom and had been registered at time of purchase, which was 1-10-87. The gun was a Smith and Wesson Model 36, .38 caliber, serial #98246. The gun, ammunition box, and all ammunition were taken by More.

More inventoried the body and found a wallet in the left rear pants pocket. The wallet contained Bothom's driver's license, one $5 bill, a Shell credit card, and miscellaneous photographs. More also removed a Timex watch and a silver ring from the body. All of these items were bagged and inventoried by More. More gave me a copy of the inventory and he took all of the personal items.

At the request of More, the body was removed at 1130 hours. More said his office would attempt to locate the relatives to notify them of the death.

REPORT #8: DRUNK IN PUBLIC ARREST

On the previously listed date and time, I was on patrol in a marked police car in the vicinity of Ball Road and Walker Street. I saw the suspect, Jodel, walking westbound. I saw that he appeared to have difficulty walking because he stumbled and almost fell, twice. I stopped my police car, parked it at the west curb, got out and walked toward the suspect, intending to check on his welfare, thinking he was either ill or drunk. When I got next to the suspect, I smelled a strong odor of alcohol; the suspect admitted to me that he had been drinking some beers at the local bar, the Fuzzy Bear Saloon. I am familiar with the bar, which is about 3 blocks away. When Jodel spoke to me, he mumbled his words so much that I could barely understand what he was saying. When I asked Jodel what time it was, he said the time was 0500 hours. In fact, the time was 1200 hours. I saw that Jodel's eyes were watery and bloodshot. His face was red and flushed. His clothing was dirty and it appeared that he had urinated in his pants. I saw what appeared to be vomit on the front of his shirt. I asked him for his driver's license. According to the license, he lived in Montebello. He had no idea how he had arrived in Anaheim. I concluded that he was intoxicated and unable to care for himself, a violation of California Penal Code Section 647 (f), drunk in public, and I arrested him.

Jodel was booked at the Anaheim city jail. He was released after remaining in detention for four hours.

REPORT #9:   PRIVATE PERSON'S ARREST-SHOPLIFTING

PROPERTY LOSS

2 - broken bottles of Blue Nun wine @ $5. 99 each $11.98

On the previously listed date and time I was dispatched to a "shoplifter in custody" at Ralph's food market.   I arrived at 1930 hours.   When I arrived, I spoke with the manager, witness #1, Lipton.   He took me to his office where the suspect was being detained by another store employee, witness #2, Earle.   The suspect had identified himself as Jerry Evans.

Lipton said he had been watching the 'floor' (shopping area) on the TV monitors in his office.   Whenever he sees someone suspicious, he radios to Earle, who then also monitors the person.   Lipton said that, via the monitors, he watched Evans walking around inside the store for about half an hour without picking up anything to examine or possibly buy.   Lipton told Earle to help Evans but Evans told Earle he didn't need any help.   After Earle left Evans, Lipton continued to watch Evans and saw him pick up two bottles of wine from a shelf in the liquor department. Lipton could not tell what type of wine it was.   Evans put the wine bottles under his shirt and walked out of the store, never stopping to pay for the items.   Earle followed Evans outside where Lipton caught up to them.   Lipton grabbed Evans by the arm, and when he did so, the bottles Evans had under his shirt fell to the ground and broke. Lipton said the broken bottles were still on the sidewalk.   Lipton, prior to my arrival, told Evans he was under arrest for theft.

Earle said he was told by Lipton via radio to watch Evans.   Earle asked Evans if he needed help and Evans said he didn't.   At that point, Evans was in the dairy section.   Earle walked away, and about 1 minute later Lipton radioed to him that Evans had just stolen two bottles of wine.   Earle saw Evans walk past two or three open check-out stations; Evans did not stop to pay for the wine.   Earle followed Evans out of the store.   When they were outside, Lipton caught up to them, and when Lipton grabbed Evans' arm, the bottles fell and broke.   Evans was brought back to the office and the police were called.

Lipton signed the private person's arrest form and told Evans he had been arrested for theft.   I handcuffed Evans.   I Mirandized Evans, but he refused to make any statements other than to give me his name, date of birth, and address.   I searched him and found $9.00 in cash on him.   Evans had no credit cards or checks on him.

While I was escorting Evans out of the store to my police car, I saw the broken wine bottles on the ground in front of the store.

I drove Evans to the jail for booking on the charge of petty theft, California Penal Code Section 488. Evans was then released on citation, # CY348769.

REPORT #10: POSSESSION OF WEAPON AND DRUGS

EVIDENCE

1 - 4" by 4" zip lock sandwich bag containing 2 ounces of a white powdery substance   Tag # 12391

2 - Smith and Wesson .357 handgun, model 177, serial number #F14722, stainless steel revolver, wooden grips, 6" barrel; 6 bullets that were used

On the previously listed date and time, I was working patrol in a marked police car. I am familiar with this area as having a high number of narcotic arrests. I was driving southbound on Main Street, approaching 15th Street, when I saw the suspect, Cassione, standing on the northwest corner. As I got closer to Cassione, I saw what appeared to be a clear plastic bag in his right hand. Cassione looked in my direction, dropped the bag on the sidewalk and started walking eastbound on 15th Street.

I parked my car, got out, and picked up the bag. I saw that it was a zip-lock sandwich bag measuring about 4 inches by 4 inches. I saw that it contained a white powdery substance resembling cocaine. I radioed for another officer and started to drive after Cassione.

I caught up to Cassione at 14th Street and Main. Officer J. Start, #3480, was the backup officer and he stood by while I arrested Cassione and handcuffed him. I arrested him for violation of Health and Safety Code Section

11350, Possession of a Controlled Substance. I searched him and found a concealed handgun in his right waistband, a violation of California Penal Code Section 12025, Possession of a Concealed Weapon. The gun was loaded with six bullets; I unloaded it. I checked Cassione for being under the influence of drugs; he wasn't. I read him his Miranda rights, but he refused to make any statements. Having arrested Cassione for the violations, I transported him to the police station. Once there, I Valtox-tested the contents of the bag; the substance proved to be cocaine.

_____
_____
_____
_____
_____
_____
_____
_____
_____
_____
_____
_____
_____

REPORT #11: WARRANT ARREST

On today's date during briefing I had been told by Detective Holt, #3489, that an arrest warrant, #A120987, had been issued for John J. Doe, a male Caucasian, with blond hair and brown eyes, height 6'1", weight 170 pounds, date of birth: January 23, 1961. The warrant was for violation of California Penal Code Section 211, Robbery. The robbery had occurred on April 15, 1997 at Sunflower Liquors, 1880 W. Temple Street, Anaheim, Case

#9201290. The suspect used a .38 caliber 2" chrome revolver in the robbery. Doe was seen driving away from the location in a white-over-blue 2-door 1985 Chevrolet Monte Carlo, license ABC 123. The car is currently registered to Jan Simple of 212 N. Bendon Way, Anaheim.

Prior to going on patrol I checked the department's field interrogation file (FI) and found a recent FI on Jane Simple, listing her current address as 3489 W. 3rd St., Anaheim.

Since Simple's address was in my patrol area, my partner, Officer Jeff Morton, #3784, and I decided to check the address to see if the suspect Doe was there. When we arrived at the location I saw parked in the driveway of the residence the car that had been used in the robbery. I drew my handgun. I saw a male matching the description of the robbery suspect run from the front yard towards the backyard. The male looked at me and my partner and I yelled "Stop!" "Police!" He stopped. I asked him his name and he told me it was John J. Doe. I confirmed his name and physical description and advised him that he was under arrest for California Penal Code Section 211, Robbery. I told him about the warrant. Officer Morton stood by while I searched Doe. In the left rear pocket I found a fully loaded Smith and Wesson .38 caliber, 2'' chrome-plated revolver. I removed the gun and unloaded it. I did not question Doe or advise him of his Miranda rights.

We drove Doe to the jail for booking on the warrant and notified Detective Holt. Holt said he would interview the suspect. When Holt arrived he took possession of the gun and ammunition.

_____
_____
_____
_____
_____
_____
_____
_____
_____
_____
_____
_____
_____
_____
_____
_____
_____

Narrative Exercises:

The following section contains a few narratives. If you want to excel rewrite all of them several times. It will help you develop a systematic way of viewing situations.

Narrative #1 - Mentally ill person

PROPERTY:

1 - Machete with red handle.   Tag #283674

On the previously listed date and time, I was on foot patrol in the area of Morris Park.   At briefing earlier this date Sergeant Donell said that several citizen complaints had been received regarding vagrants living in the park. The vagrants had accosted and harassed citizens who were using the park facilities.

While I was walking along the west parkway I saw Miles talking to an unknown male. The male motioned with his hand for me to come to him. He told me that he felt that Miles was a danger to the public because he had a machete that he was waving around and he did not seem to be coherent.   I requested another officer to assist me, and Officer Ertin was dispatched to my location. I asked the unknown male to remain at the scene so I could obtain further information, but he refused to stay and left the area.

I saw the machete on a park bench, about 5-7 feet from where Miles was standing. I started to talk to Miles and quickly formed the opinion that he was possibly mentally ill. He did not seem to know where he was or what day it was, and much of his speech was slurred and incoherent. He told me that he had tried to kill himself several months ago.   After he told me about the attempted suicide, his speech became incoherent again and I couldn't get any further information from him. He made several statements that caused me to be concerned for citizens using the park. He claimed the park was his and he knew he had to "rid the park of the beasts who destroy it." He also said he had already "eliminated the undesirables" but would not go further into what he meant. Once again he became incoherent. While he was talking, he frequently hit his face with his fist and shouted incoherent phrases at passersby.

Miles' appearance was unkempt. He smelled of body odor and his clothes were dirty and sour-smelling. His hair and beard were matted and dirty. Although he was wearing a shoe and sock on his right foot, his left foot was bare, and I didn't see any shoes or socks in the immediate viewing area.

Once Officer Ertin arrived I took Miles into custody under the authority of Welfare and Institutions Code Section 5150 as a Danger to Others.   When I attempted to handcuff Miles, he became violent to such a degree that both Officer Ertin and I had to push him to the ground in an attempt to place his arms behind his back. He kicked at me and was yelling "I'm God." and "You'll pay in hell."   Neither Miles, nor Officer Ertin or I were injured in the fight. I took the machete and booked it under tag # 283674, for destruction.   I drove Miles to Charter Hospital, 12687 Cherry Avenue in Long Beach for 72-hour observation. Case closed.

Narrative #2 - Theft

On the previously listed date and time, I was dispatched to the noted address regarding a theft. When I arrived at 1625 hours, the victim, Delroy, told me the following: he had parked his vehicle, a 1989 Jeep Cherokee, California license Y345OPO, in his driveway at 1545 hours. He left the TV and phone on the backseat of the vehicle and left the cash in the glove compartment. The vehicle's driver's side window was rolled down and the driver's side door was left unlocked.

Delroy said he had not intended to be inside his house so long. He lost track of time. About 30 minutes after he went into the house, he remembered that the items were in the vehicle and the window was down and the door was unlocked. When he returned to the vehicle at about 1615 hours he discovered the items were gone. He did not see or hear anything unusual. Delroy had no idea who might've committed the theft and said he would support prosecution if the suspect was located.

Before I left the area I went to the following addresses in an attempt to locate witnesses: 4356, 4357, 4358, 4359 Oakdale. No one came to the door at any of the addresses so I left my business card with a note requesting the resident at each address to call me.

Case closed pending additional information.

Narrative #2a - Residential burglary

On the previously listed date and time, I was on patrol in a marked patrol car in the area of 6000 Leaf Drive when the victim, Brown, flagged me down. He told me that he had just arrived home and discovered that his house had been broken into. He showed me the house, which is a 1-story stucco building with three bedrooms, kitchen, den, and two baths, with an attached two-car garage. The house has no alarm. The address is 6000 Leaf Drive.

Brown said he had arrived home at about 1000 hours from a three-day vacation. After driving into his garage he noticed the door that leads into the house from the garage interior was splintered and leaning against the garage doorframe. He walked into the house and discovered it had been burglarized.

Brown took me on a tour of the house and showed me the desk in the den where the television and laptop computer had been when he went on vacation. I could see an outline of dust on the desk and I could see where two rectangular items had rested. Brown took me on a room-by-room tour; it seemed that the rest of the house had not been disturbed.

Brown said he lived in the house by himself and no one had permission to be in the house other than his neighbor, James Blount, (DOB 2-4-43), 5800 Leaf Drive, (714) 598-8459. Mr. Blount had keys to the house and would check on the house for the victim whenever the victim was gone. Brown said he had no idea who might've committed the burglary and said he would support prosecution if the suspect is found.

_____
_____
_____
_____
_____
_____
_____
_____
_____
_____
_____
_____
_____
_____
_____
_____
_____
_____
_____
_____
_____
_____

Narrative #3 - Commercial robbery

PROPERTY LOSS

$250 cash, U.S. currency, miscellaneous bills

EVIDENCE

1 - Videotape of robbery - Evidence Tag # 23980

On the previously listed date and time, I was dispatched to the Sav-On Drugstore at 1278 N. Brookhurst regarding a robbery that had just occurred. While en route, I was given the description of the two suspects, their vehicle, and direction of travel. That information appears on the front page of this report.

I arrived at 2235 hours and spoke with the victim, Brown. I confirmed the suspect and vehicle descriptions I had previously been given, and confirmed that both suspects were armed with handguns. Brown said the robbery occurred about 5 minutes before I arrived.

I requested that dispatch advise Orange County Communications of the robbery and that a general broadcast be made alerting all Orange County law enforcement agencies to the suspect and vehicle descriptions. That broadcast was made at 2245 hours, broadcast #22-458-23.

Brown told me he had been working behind the photo counter at about 2230 hours. He was in the process of closing his cash register and was counting the money on the counter. To the best of his knowledge there were no customers in the store. The only other employee was Smith. Brown looked up to see the two suspects enter the north doors and immediately walk to the photo counter. He said that he had never seen the two suspects before but felt threatened because they were wearing bulky clothing and both looked at the cash on the counter. He said that as the suspects approached the counter they took guns out from underneath their bulky jackets and pointed the guns at him.

Suspect #1 said to him "Give me all the money or I'll blow your damn head off." Suspect #2 never said anything. Brown said both suspects appeared to be nervous because their foreheads were sweating and their gun-hands shook. Brown said, "I was so scared - I thought for sure they would shoot me." He handed all the money on the counter to Suspect #1 and the two suspects ran out the north doors and in an unknown direction from there. Brown then called the police.

Brown said he had enough time as the suspects approached the counter to push the auto-record button to the closed-circuit camera to capture the robbery on tape. I watched the videotape and because it was in color I could see the suspects' clothing description, etc., provided by Brown appeared to be accurate. He gave me the tape and I booked it into evidence. He said that the suspects did not touch the counter top. Brown said he is experienced with handguns and he believed the guns were .38 caliber blue-steel revolvers with 4" barrels. Brown said he would recognize both suspects if he saw them again and would support prosecution.

Witness Smith told me that at the time the robbery occurred, she had been standing near the pharmacy, about 35 feet away from the photo counter where Brown had been counting the money. She saw the two suspects enter through the north doors and thought it was strange that the two were wearing such heavy, bulky clothing because the weather was so hot. She did not think that either suspect saw her since she was partially hidden by the pharmacy counter. She watched as the suspects walked to the photo counter and pulled out their guns. She saw the suspects point the guns at Brown but could not hear what the suspects said to Brown. She did not see their faces and only saw the suspects from the rear. She did not think she could recognize the suspect if she saw them again. The description she provided of the suspects' clothing matched the description the victim had given to me and what I saw on the video tape, but she added that the suspect who did all the talking (suspect #1) had on a gold earring in his left earlobe.

Witness Smith said that after the suspects left the store through the north doors, she looked around the corner to see the suspects get into the vehicle described on page 1. She provided the description of the suspect vehicle but was unable to see a rear license plate because the lighting was poor. She said that suspect #2 drove the vehicle north on Brookhurst and then out of sight. She would be able to recognize the vehicle if she saw it again and would testify. Case closed pending review by detectives.

_____
_____
_____
_____
_____
_____
_____
_____
_____
_____
_____
_____
_____
_____
_____
_____
_____
_____
_____
_____
_____

Narrative #4 - Domestic violence

INJURIES   Blackened right eye and cheek of victim (photo attached)   Tag # 19728

On the previously listed date and time, I was dispatched to the noted address regarding a fight between husband and wife.   Officer Erin was the assigned follow-up officer. When I arrived the victim, M. Brown, met me at the front door of the residence. She said she had called the police because her husband, E. Brown, had struck her in the face with his hand. While Officer Erin talked to the suspect, I spoke with the victim.

The victim told me that she had arrived home from work at about 1640 hours. She immediately discovered that her husband had not gone to work today but had stayed home and had apparently been drinking. She believed that he had been drinking because he smelled of alcohol and there were several empty beer cans strewn about the living room. When she went into the living room, she saw her husband sleeping on the couch. She woke him up and he immediately got mad at her for doing so.

She said he called her a "bitch" and hit her with an open hand on the right side of her face. She said he had pushed her before but had never struck her like he did today.   She said she did nothing to provoke the injury.   She refused medical aid.   She said she wanted him arrested and would testify.

I could see swelling and black-and-blue bruising on the right side of her face. Her right eyelid and the skin under the eye had already started to turn black- and-blue. I took a Polaroid photo of the injury and that photo is included with this report.

I looked into the living room and saw several chairs, tables, and knickknacks strewn about in disarray, which gave me the impression that a fight may have occurred.   There were five empty Budweiser beer cans on the living room floor.

I read E. Brown the Miranda Advisement, Form #347. He said "Yeah, I'll tell ya what happened", and signed the form waiving his rights. He agreed with the statements of the victim, up to the point where the victim said she had received her injuries. E. Brown said she had struck him first, hitting him two or three times on the face and chest with her fist, and he struck her while trying to defend himself. He said "Yeah, I called her a bitch because she is a bitch and always complains about my drinking. If she wouldn't bug me all the time, I wouldn't have to keep her in line." He admitted to drinking "about" five beers earlier today but at the time of our interview showed no signs of intoxication.

I did not see any signs of redness or injury on E. Brown's face.   He refused medical aid.

Before we left the scene I gave the victim a copy of Form #4587, entitled "Notification to Victims of Domestic Violence", which listed shelter and counseling information, right to arrest, and the report number of the incident.

I placed E. Brown under arrest for violation of CPC 273.5, Spousal Abuse, and transported him to the jail for booking. The suspect was held for $50,000 bail.

I reviewed our police department records for prior reports regarding domestic violence involving these parties.   I located two other reports: DR#04-8970 dated 10-23-04 and DR#05-9983 dated 11-21-05. Copies of those reports are attached.

91

Case closed by arrest.

Narrative #5 - Assault and battery

INJURIES   Victim had ½" cut on lip (photo attached) Tag # 109834

On the previously listed date and time, I was on patrol in a marked police car in the area of 6000 Lime St. when I saw a group of at least five people blocking the street. I stopped to investigate and saw that Victim Doyle and Suspect Toth were fighting on the ground. I pulled them apart and requested a follow-up officer.

I saw that Doyle was bleeding from the lip. He refused medical care and told me the fight started when Toth got upset with him when his baseball went into Toth's backyard. Doyle said he was in his own backyard playing ball with his dog, Fido. He had thrown the ball too high and the ball flew into the suspect's backyard. Doyle went to Toth's home and asked him if he could retrieve the ball. Toth became verbally abusive calling him an "ass" and started to push Doyle off the property. Doyle told Toth to stop pushing him and with that Toth punched the victim in the face with his fist. The two began fighting and ended up in the street with several neighbors standing by watching. Doyle said he never hit the suspect or called him any names.

Doyle said he and the suspect have known each other for about six years and have never liked each other. The two have been involved in two or three arguments over the years but the arguments never escalated into a fight. Doyle said he was not seriously injured. He refused medical aid. He did want the suspect arrested for assault and battery. Doyle said he would support prosecution. I took a Polaroid photo of the victim's injury and that photo is attached to this report.

Once Officer Start, #3489, arrived I had him stand by while I interviewed the suspect. After the suspect read and signed the attached Miranda advisement waiver form, he told me that he had known the victim for about five years. The victim and he have never gotten along because of an old girlfriend, Margie Parsons, whom they both liked and both had dated. The incident that started today began when the victim came to the suspect's home wanting to get a baseball in the suspect's backyard. The suspect insisted that the name-calling began when the victim called him an "ass" and "white trash" and punched him. The suspect stated that he only defended himself by striking back, hitting the victim in the face.

Witness #1, Mayer, walked up to me and told me that she had seen the fight. She said she had been in her driveway, which is next door to the suspect's home. She heard some yelling coming from the suspect's home and heard the suspect call the victim an "ass." She saw the suspect push the second victim, possibly three times before the victim even began to defend himself. She said the victim repeatedly told the suspect to stop pushing him but the suspect continued to push and shove the victim. She saw the suspect use his right fist to punch the victim in the face, which knocked the victim to the ground. She added that, as a neighbor, she knows both parties. She said she would be willing to testify.

I asked three or four additional witnesses what they saw but only Witness #2, Boyer, would talk to me. Boyer said he was talking to Mayer in her driveway when he heard Doyle and Toth arguing. He looked in the direction of the suspect's home and heard the suspect call the victim an "ass." He saw thesuspect push the victim at least once and then the suspect punched the victim in the face, knocking him to the ground. He never saw the victim attempt to hit the suspect but he did hear the victim tell the suspect to "leave me alone." Mayer pointed at the suspect and said that he was the aggressor. Mayer then pointed to the victim and said that he was the victim. Mayer said that he would be willing to testify.

At 1445 hours I had the victim place the suspect under private person's arrest and accepted the suspect into my custody for booking at the jail. I transported the suspect to the jail at 1455 hours and I booked him for violation of CPC 240-242, Assault and Battery. Booking was completed at 1645 hours and the suspect was released on a citation, #459870.

Case closed by arrest.

Narrative #6 - Assault with a deadly weapon

INJURY

1 - cut on victim's forehead, between 1 inch and 1 ½ inches long(Photo of injury) Tag # 12577

EVIDENCE

1 - Baseball bat, brown wood, blood stains on upper half

1 - Men's T-shirt, size extra large, blood-stained (victim's)   Tag # 12579

On the previously listed date and time, I was dispatched to the listed address regarding a fight in the parking lot of Denny's restaurant. Officer S. Smalley,#24578, was assigned as my follow-up officer. I arrived at about 2345 hours and Officer Smalley arrived at about 2346 hours.

When I arrived, I saw the victim, Noe, sitting on the pavement in front of the restaurant, holding his head in his hands. I saw blood coming from his head and it appeared to me that he had a 1" to 1 ½" cut on his forehead. I requested the paramedics and provided a bandage for the victim. When I asked him what had happened, he pointed north, towards the suspect's vehicle, a black Ford Mustang, California License I LIK IT, which was about 25 feet away from where I was standing and the victim was sitting. The victim said the person seated behind the wheel was the person who had hit him with a bat. I could see the suspect, Manley, seated behind the wheel of the vehicle.

I had Officer Smalley drive to the rear of the suspect's car and use the police car to block the car from leaving. Officer Smalley and I had our weapons drawn and I told the suspect to get out of the vehicle. Manley got out of the vehicle and while doing so said "The jerk has been seeing my ex-wife and he's been asking for it - I should've killed him."   I handcuffed the suspect and placed him in the back of my patrol car. I looked in the back seat of the suspect vehicle and I saw a baseball bat. The bat had a red substance, possibly blood, on it. Officer Smalley and I searched the suspect's car but found no other weapons or contraband. I took the baseball bat out of the car to book as evidence.

The paramedics arrived at 2348 hours and attended to the victim. Paramedic Smith, #2456, stated that the victim probably had a concussion and would be transported to InterCity Hospital, 2356 Garfield, Alhambra. I took the victim's T-shirt as evidence because of the bloodstains on it. Before the victim was transported to the hospital, I took a Polaroid photo of his injury.

Officer Smalley checked the restaurant and surrounding areas for witnesses but was able to locate only one witness, Nelson. Nelson said that she had been driving northbound on Light St. when she saw Manley and Noe in the parking lot of the restaurant. She heard them yelling at each other but couldn't hear what they were saying. She saw the suspect hit the victim once on the head, with a baseball bat, and saw the victim fall down. She parked across the street and called the police on her cellular phone and waited until the police arrived. She pointed to Manley and said he was the person she had seen hit the victim. She said she would testify.

After I advised the suspect of his rights per Miranda, he signed the waiver, Form #5298, Advisement of Rights Waiver (attached). He said he knew that the victim had been dating his ex-wife and he didn't like the fact that she was dating anyone so soon after their divorce. The suspect said he followed the victim's car when the victim left the ex-wife's house this evening, at about 2300 hours. The victim drove to the restaurant and went inside for about ½ hr. The suspect waited for the victim outside and when the victim opened his car door, the suspect walked up to him yelled "son of a bitch" at him and then hit him once with the bat. The suspect appeared angry while he was telling me the story, because he was red faced and yelling. He added "If you give me the chance, I'll kill him - my wife is too good for him."

Officer Smalley drove the suspect to the jail for booking for violation of CPC

245 (a) (2), Assault with a Deadly Weapon. The suspect was held on $35,000 bail. I booked the bat, shirt and photo into evidence. The suspect's vehicle was left locked in the parking lot of the restaurant. The vehicle is registered to the suspect.

At 0055 hours on January 3, 1995, I went to the hospital to check on the victim's condition. He was conscious and said he would remain in the hospital overnight. He had received a concussion and required six stitches in his forehead. He said that he would see to it that a copy of his medical report was forwarded to the police department to be included in this report.

He told me that he didn't know the suspect had followed him to the restaurant. He knew from talking to the suspect's ex-wife, Mary Ann Manley, that the suspect could be very jealous. He had been dating the ex-wife for two to three months and this incident was the first time that he had had any problem with the suspect. When he walked out of the restaurant the suspect yelled his name and then hit him on the head with the bat. The victim said he would support prosecution.

Case closed by arrest.

_____
_____
_____
_____
_____
_____
_____
_____
_____
_____
_____
_____
_____
_____

Narrative #7 - Drunk in public arrest

On the previously listed date and time, Officer Smith and I were dispatched to The Sports Bar at 1234 E. Levy Street, regarding a disturbance. We arrived at 0132 hours, entered the bar and spoke to Bill Night, who said he had called the police. Night pointed to the suspect, Williams. Night said that Williams had come into the bar about one hour earlier, already intoxicated. Williams had asked Night to serve him liquor and Night refused. Night told Williams to leave because he was disturbing other customers by being loud and obnoxious. Night had seen Williams approach two or three bar customers and ask them to buy him a drink, and when they refused, Williams yelled at them and called them names like "asshole" and "butthead." Night said that he wanted Williams removed from the property for the remainder of the evening.

Officer Smith and I escorted Williams outside. I spoke to Williams and when he replied he slurred his words. Williams admitted to drinking a "few beers" earlier this date. I smelled a strong odor of an unknown type of alcohol on his breath. His clothing was in disarray and dirty. His face was red and flushed and his eyes were bloodshot. He could not stand without some assistance.

I arrested Williams for drunk in public, violation of California Penal Code Section 647(f). I drove him to the jail, where he was held for a four-hour detainment and then released.

Case closed by arrest.

Narrative #8 - Rape

EVIDENCE

1 - Pink ladies blouse, size 34   Tag # 29057

1 - Pair ladies Levis, size medium   Tag # 29058

1 - Victim rape kit   Tag # 29059

6 - Photos of victim   Tag # 29060

On the previously listed date and time, I was dispatched to a pay phone located at 112 S. Mertle Street, Milepost Park, regarding a 911 call received from the public telephone at that location. Dispatcher D. Lytle told me that the call had been made by an unidentified female who was crying and said she had been raped. The caller had then hung up the phone.

I arrived at about 2245 hours and found the victim , Pauley, seated next to the pay phone, crying. When I asked her if she had called 911, she said she had done so. Her left cheek was red and bruised and her blouse was dirty and torn. She said she had been raped by two armed male Hispanics who then dropped her off at the park. She provided the descriptions of the two suspects and their vehicle. The descriptions appear on page one of this report. At 2253 hours, a general broadcast (GB#4568709) was made to all Orange County law enforcement agencies regarding the suspects' description and their vehicle.

The victim told me the following: she had been shopping alone at the Town City Mall, 1209 Munley Street, Alhambra, until approximately 2030 hours. She was walking back to her car, which was parked in the southeast parking lot, when she was approached by the two suspects. Suspect #1, the driver, drove his vehicle next to her and showed her a gun and told her "Get in the car or you're dead." She got into the back seat with suspect #2. Suspect #2 also had a gun and pointed it at her while suspect #1 drove to an unknown location. She was forced to lie down on the floorboard and could not see where the suspect drove. She could not provide further information about the guns that both suspects had other than to say both guns were chrome.

She said they drove around for about ten minutes and then suspect #1 stopped the car. Both suspects pulled her from the car. She saw they were on an unlit dirt road in an area that she didn't recognize. While suspect #1 pointed the gun at her, suspect #2 began to tear her clothing off. Suspect #2 kept telling her "Just do as we say and you won't get hurt." She was crying and screaming. Suspect #2 hit her on her left cheek with his fist, knocking her to the ground. She believed that she lost consciousness for a few minutes because when she woke up suspect #2 was lying on top of her, raping her. The suspect had inserted his penis into her vagina and ejaculated. Suspect #1 was still holding the gun and kept it pointed at her while suspect #2 raped her.

Both suspects then left the area in their vehicle, leaving her stranded. She managed to find her blouse and pants but could not find her panties, bra or shoes. She found her purse next to her clothing. All items were still in her purse. After finding her clothing and getting dressed, she walked for about 15 minutes until she came to the telephone in the park. She said that she would probably be able to recognize the suspects if she saw them again and would testify.

I told the victim that it would be helpful to our investigation if she would consent to a rape examination and explained to her what the examination involved. She said she would do so and I drove her to Intercommunity Hospital, 12034 Denton Ave. We arrived at the hospital at about 2355 hours. Before the victim underwent the examination, I took six Polaroid photographs of her. Dr. Marsha Gordon treated the victim. Dr. Gordon completed the rape kit and sealed it at 0100 hours. I took custody of the rape kit and later booked it into the evidence refrigerator. A copy of the doctor's report is attached to this report.

The victim called her sister from the hospital. The sister, Miriam Renton, brought additional clothing to the hospital for the victim. I took custody of the blouse and pants the victim had been wearing at the time of the assault and booked them and the photographs into evidence.

The victim consented to accompanying her sister and me to the general vicinity of the park in an attempt to locate the area where the rape had occurred. We drove in my marked police car to an unnamed dirt road that is ¼ mile east of the park, but the victim was unable to say with any certainty that this was the area where the attack occurred. I was unable to locate any of the victim's missing clothing or any signs that the attack had occurred in this area.

The victim stated she wanted to get her car from the shopping center parking lot, so at 0145 hours I drove her and her sister back to the shopping center and found her car. I checked the area around her car, a 1995 Honda Prelude, California license B BODY, for evidence and found none.

Case open; refer to investigation.

Narrative #9 - Suicide

EVIDENCE

1 - Suicide note Tag # 129799

1 - Last Will and Testament   Tag # 129800

On the previously listed date and time, Officer J. Smally, #3457, and I were dispatched to the listed address regarding a dead body. Dispatcher C. Quinton stated she had also dispatched the paramedics. We arrived at 1135 hours. We were met at the curb by J. Nome, who pointed to the house at 22390 S. Oakleaf Drive, next door to her own residence. She said while she was in her house, she heard one gunshot, which sounded like it had come from her neighbor's house, the one at 22390 S. Oakleaf Drive. She went next door, to 22390, saw that the garage door was up, and found her neighbor seated in a chair in the garage. She said she thought her neighbor was dead because he wasn't moving at all, there was blood on his head, and he didn't seem to be breathing. She touched nothing. She immediately called the police.

Officer Smally and I went to the front of the attached garage of the residence at 22390 S. Oakleaf Drive. The garage door was up.   We saw a white male subject seated upright in a chair in the center of the garage. Nome identified the person in the chair as her neighbor, John L. Langley. I checked the man's neck for a pulse and checked for breathing, but detected neither. I looked at both eyes and saw that the pupils were dilated.   It appeared that he had a wound in his left temple because there was blood coming from that area. A handgun was in the victim's left hand and there were blood splatters on the victim's left hand and on the gun.   The left hand and gun rested in his lap. Officer Smally and I checked the rest of the house for additional people and found none. The house appeared neat and tidy.   There was one car, a 1989 Cadillac Seville, California license RUGGED, parked in the driveway.   It was locked and appeared untouched.

The paramedics arrived at 1137 hours. Paramedic J. Neery, #289, pronounced the victim dead at 1138 hours.   I requested a deputy coroner and a crime scene investigator at 1140 hours.

Nome said that the victim lived alone and had been depressed for quite some time due to ill health. She said that the victim suffered from bone cancer and had been in pain for a number of months. She had last spoken to the victim at about 0730 hours this date when she saw him picking up his newspaper in his driveway. She said 'hello' to him. He asked her if she would watch his dog, Mopsie, because he might be gone for a few weeks or longer. She said she would look after the dog as she often did when he would leave. She did not know if the victim had any family or relatives who lived locally. The dog was in the backyard. Nome said she would care for the dog until other arrangements could be made.

When I walked into the kitchen, I saw two pieces of paper on the kitchen table. One of the pieces of paper, approximately 3" x 5", was a hand-printed note, with the victim's name written at the bottom, as a signature would be. The note read "I can't take the pain and loneliness anymore. Please see to it that

Mopsie is cared for by my neighbor." I collected the original note as evidence. The other piece of paper was approximately 8½" x 11" sheet, typewritten, with the words "Last Will and Testament of John J. Langley" typed at the top of the page. The note said that Langley was leaving all his possessions to his sister, Mary Jones, 11445 Mountain Road, South Fork, Idaho 89214, telephone (601)257-7954. There were four typewritten paragraphs, and a handwritten date and the apparent signature of the victim at the bottom of the page. I collected the apparent will as evidence. On the kitchen counter was an opened box of ammunition; there were six bullets missing from the box, which had contained 50 bullets.

Crime scene investigator L. Golton, #289, arrived at 1148 hours and took photographs of the scene. Refer to his supplemental report.

In the kitchen, on the counter, I found two prescription bottles of medication, 1 bottle each of Prozac and Demerol, in the victim's name. By calling the pharmacy phone number listed on the label of the bottles, I was able to obtain the name of the treating physician (Dr. John Adler). I called Dr. Adler, 12098 Downey Ave., Downey, 213-586-3746, who confirmed that the victim was suffering from bone cancer. Dr. Adler said he had last seen the victim on the 19th of this month. Dr. Adler also confirmed that the victim had been in extreme pain and was extremely depressed the last time he saw him.

Coroner's Investigator W. Bueller, #12098, arrived at 1235 hours. I told him what I had learned from Nome and the doctor, and confirmed that nothing had been touched or moved. Investigator Bueller examined the scene with me and confirmed that the death appeared to be a suicide. He examined the handgun found in the victim's left hand. It was a .38 caliber revolver, Smith and Wesson Model 15, serial #292876K. He said that one bullet had been fired from the gun. An inventory of the victim's property was conducted in my presence. Items retained by Investigator Bueller were (1) the victim's wallet containing $35.00 cash, the victim's driver's license, two credit cards, and miscellaneous photographs; (2) a Timex watch; (3) a white metal ring; and (4) both bottles of prescription medication. The gun and all other items were kept by the coroner's investigator. I received an inventory of those items retained by Coroner's Investigator Bueller. That inventory is attached to this report. I showed Bueller the will and the suicide note, and provided a copy of both for his report when I got back to the station. A coroner's van arrived at 1425 hours and the body was removed at 1435 hours. Investigator Bueller said that an autopsy would be performed the following day and I could get the final written results in two weeks.

I requested that dispatch check the registration of the vehicle in the driveway and of the handgun. According to Department of Motor Vehicles records, the vehicle was registered to the victim, and Department of Justice firearms records showed the handgun as being registered to the victim.

Case open, pending results of the autopsy.

_____

_____

_____

_____

_____

_____

_____

Narrative #10 - Suicide

EVIDENCE

1 - Suicide note Tag # 28057

On the previously listed date and time, I was dispatched to the noted address regarding an attempted suicide. Dispatcher P. Rollins told me that the female apparently attempting suicide had called on the 911 line and was crying. When Rollins asked what the problem was, the female said that she "wanted to die" and had taken "some pills." The telephone connection was then broken. Rollins said that she had obtained the address where the call had originated through the 911 operator. Rollins continued to call the phone number while I was en route to the noted address, but she got the busy tone every time she called.

The backup officer assigned to assist on this call was Officer Wefton, #498, and we both arrived at the same time, approximately 1457 hours. We went to the front door of the residence and knocked several times, each time calling out "Police." We tried to open the front door but it was locked. We did not get any response to our knocks and yells, so we walked to the rear door of the residence and found it unlocked. We entered and called out several more times "Police." I heard some moaning and, following the sound, I found the victim, Sally Ann Porter, on the floor of the front bathroom. She was semi-conscious but was unable to answer my questions about what had happened to her. I saw 4 medicine bottles on the floor and there were pills, possibly from those bottles, strewn about on the floor. Because I believed that she might have ingested some of the contents of those bottles, I requested the paramedics. I made the request at approximately 1500 hours. I saw no injuries to her body, and it appeared that she had vomited an unknown substance onto her blouse.

While I stayed with Porter, Officer Wefton searched the remainder of the house to see if anyone else was there. He didn't find anyone. During his search of the house, he found a note on the kitchen table. He believed it had been written by Porter because it had her name as the signature. The note said that she wanted to die and that she had no reason to live anymore. A copy of the note is attached to this report. I booked the note into evidence under Tag #28057.

The paramedics arrived at approximately 1505 hours and began to treat Victim Porter. The paramedics took the medicine bottles, labeled as Valium, Codeine, Aspirin, and Paxil, to the hospital. Porter was transported to Anaheim Memorial Hospital for further treatment.

We arrived at Anaheim Memorial Hospital at approximately 1535 hours, and a few minutes later I spoke to the attending physician, Dr. M. Yaden. He told me that Porter had ingested an unknown amount of prescription medications, pills believed to be Valium and Codeine, from the bottles that I had found in the front bathroom. He believed that Porter had tried to commit suicide. He said he had talked to Dr. W. Carter, the psychiatrist who had been treating Porter and who had prescribed the Valium for her. Dr. Carter had not prescribed the Codeine for Porter. Dr. Yaden gave me Dr. Carter's phone number and address: (714) 849-0989, 1290 West 5th St., Anaheim. The prescription bottle containing Codeine bore the name of Dr. V. Opty as the prescriber. I couldn't talk with Dr. Opty because she was out of town. Dr. Opty's phone number and address are: (714) 234-9909, 239 Midvale Ave., Anaheim.

I told Dr. Yaden about the telephone call that Porter had made on 911 and showed him the apparent suicide note.

Drs. Yaden and Carter agreed that Porter should be housed in the hospital psychiatric ward as a Danger to Self, pursuant to Welfare and Institutions Code 5150.

At 1559 hours, Porter was left in the care and custody of Dr. Yaden.

Narrative #11 - Private Person's Arrest

PROPERTY LOSS

1 - Set of six wrenches, in a single package, Sears Craftsman brand, recovered; photo attached $79.00

EVIDENCE

1- Videotape of the theft   Tag # 20001

On the previously listed date and time, Officer J. Smith, #212 and I were dispatched to the noted address regarding a shoplifter in custody. I arrived at about 1930 hours. When I arrived, I spoke with witness Jones, who is the Security Manager for the store. He said that the suspect, Morales, and the other witness, Banlon, were in the Security Manager's office. He told me the following: he had been working in his office in the store at about 1856 hours this date and saw the suspect, Morales, on the closed-circuit TV which is kept in his office. He saw Morales was in the automotive department and that Morales kept looking around as if to see if anyone was looking at him. Jones radioed to his assistant, witness Banlon, and told him to watch Morales.

While Banlon made his way to the automotive department, Jones continued to watch Morales on the closed-circuit TV. Jones turned on the time-lapse video recorder and recorded the actions of Morales. Jones watched the suspect walk around the automotive tool section, take a set of wrenches off a shelf in the tool section as he walked past the shelf, and stuff the set of wrenches down the front of his pants, near the crotch area. The suspect frequently looked around as if to see whether anyone was watching him. The suspect then slowly made his way to the front of the store, walking past three open and staffed cash register stations. The suspect made no attempt to pay for the item he had stuffed in his pants. The suspect continued to walk, going out the north front doors, with Banlon approximately 6 feet behind him.

Once the suspect and Banlon were outside the store and on the sidewalk, Banlon tapped the suspect on his shoulder and asked him to return to the store. The suspect cooperated and walked back into the store with Banlon, to the Security Manager's office. Once the suspect was inside the office, Jones asked him if he knew why he had been stopped. The suspect replied "O.K., you got me - here it is", removed the package of wrenches from inside the front of his pants, and handed the package of wrenches to Banlon.

Jones told me that he wanted the suspect arrested for petty theft and would support prosecution of the suspect for that crime. Jones then took me to the Security Manager's Office, where witness Banlon was detaining the suspect. The suspect remained in the Security Manager's office with Jones and Officer Smith while I then interviewed witness Banlon. Banlon said that his manager, Jones, had told him to watch the suspect, and he did so. Banlon said he discreetly followed the suspect around in the automotive section for about five minutes and then saw the suspect pick up a set of wrenches and place it in his pants.

Banlon followed the suspect out through the store's front doors, and the suspect did not stop to pay for the wrenches. The suspect made no statements until he was brought to the office and Jones confronted him.

Banlon heard the suspect say "O.K., you got me - here it is" and saw the suspect remove the wrenches from his pants.

Both witnesses said that they had never seen the suspect in the store before. Both witnesses identified the wrenches as belonging to their store, and pointed out the store inventory/price tag still in place on the package.

I took a Polaroid photo of the package of wrenches and returned the wrenches to Jones. The photo of the property is attached to this report. I watched the videotape of the theft and the tape clearly showed the suspect place an item down the front of his pants, then turn and leave the store without paying for that item. I took the tape as evidence and booked it under Evidence Tag #20001.

I provided the suspect with Form 238, Advisement of Rights. I read and explained those rights to him, and he signed the form, signifying that he understood his rights. He refused to talk with me about the charges against him. I searched the suspect and found $3.00 in U.S. currency. I found no other means by which the suspect could have paid for the item he had taken.

Jones told the suspect that he was under arrest for theft, violation of California Penal Code section 484/488. I transported the suspect to the jail for booking. The suspect was later released on Citation No. DE239479.

Case closed by arrest.

_____
_____
_____
_____
_____
_____
_____
_____
_____
_____
_____
_____
_____
_____
_____
_____
_____

Narrative #12 - Warrant arrest

On the previously listed date and time, I was on patrol in a marked police car, driving westbound in the 6000 block of Lincoln Avenue, when I saw the suspect, Smith, driving a blue 1969 Chevrolet El Camino, California license 230TTT, ahead of me and also westbound on Lincoln, approaching the intersection of Lincoln and Valley View. Smith failed to stop his vehicle at the stop sign at the corner of westbound Lincoln and northbound Valley View before he turned northbound onto Valley View. The failure to stop was a violation of California Vehicle Code section 22450. I was directly behind Smith when I saw the violation. I stopped my car at that stop sign and then turned right onto northbound Valley View. I was again directly behind Smith.

I turned on my patrol car's overhead lights and siren and Smith immediately pulled his vehicle to the east curb of northbound Valley View. When I walked up to his vehicle, I saw that he was alone. He was perspiring heavily on the forehead, even though the driver's side window was down and the outside temperature was about 60 degrees (Fahrenheit). I asked him if something was wrong and he said "No." I told him why I had stopped him (failure to stop at the stop sign) and I asked to see his driver's license. He said that he had forgotten to bring his license with him. He said the vehicle was registered to him. I asked him to get out of his vehicle, and he did. He told me his name and date of birth and I radioed that information to dispatch. Dispatch told me that there was a warrant for Smith's arrest for burglary, California Penal Code section 459.

Officer R. Smolten, #3736, who was assigned as my follow-up officer, arrived approximately two minutes later. I then told Smith he was under arrest pursuant to the warrant, and I handcuffed him. He offered no resistance, and said "I knew my luck couldn't last forever." I searched him and found nothing except a wallet containing $5.00 cash. Smith asked that I let his wife pick up the vehicle instead of having it towed. I told him he could call his wife from the police station to arrange to have the vehicle picked up.

I cited Smith for the stop sign violation, Citation #493766. I drove Smith to the Cypress City Jail for booking on the warrant. Case closed by arrest.

Warrant #384590098. Issued 4-7-95 by Judge D. Bice, Orange County Superior Court (West), charging violation of California Penal Code section 459, Burglary. Bail $25,000.00

Narrative #13 - Possession of a controlled substance

EVIDENCE

1 - 2" x 2" clear cellophane baggie containing white powder, 1.2 grams   Tag # 38456

2 - 2" x 2" empty, clear cellophane baggies with white residue   Tag # 38457

On the previously listed date and time, Officer Verry, #456 and I were on patrol in a marked police car in the 2100 block of State College Blvd., when I saw the suspect, Reynolds, driving a 1979 red Chevrolet Corvette, California license 202HJH. I saw the car make a U-turn in front of the driveway to the fire station at 2150 State College Boulevard. That U-turn was a violation of California Vehicle Code (CVC) Section 22104.

I turned on my patrol car's overhead lights and siren and Reynolds stopped his car at the north curb line of State College Blvd. When I walked up to Reynolds as he sat in his car, I saw that he was alone. He appeared to be quite nervous because when I asked for his driver's license he fumbled for his wallet and started to sweat profusely on his hands and forehead. As he opened up his wallet a cellophane baggie, containing a white powder, fell out onto the pavement. I looked at the baggie and then looked at Reynolds. He said, "I don't know how that got there, officer- it isn't mine." I said to him "It was in your wallet." Reynolds said "I don't know if I want to talk to you now." I looked at Reynolds' nose and saw white dust particles at the opening of his nostrils. I looked into his nostrils and saw white dust particles clinging to his nose hairs. Based upon my training and experience, the substance in the baggie looked like cocaine, and I know that cocaine is commonly sniffed or "snorted" into the nose. I had Reynolds get out of the car, handcuffed him and told him that he was under arrest for Possession of a Controlled Substance, a violation of California Health and Safety (H&S) Code Section 11350.

While Officer Verry watched Reynolds, I searched the interior of Reynolds' car. I found two more baggies under the driver's seat. They were of the same type that Reynolds had dropped. Both bags were empty, but had a white residue on the inside.

Reynolds' car was towed for storage pursuant to CVC 22651 (h)(1).   The registration showed that it was registered to him.

Officer Verry and I drove Reynolds to the station for booking. When we arrived, I immediately Valtox-tested the contents of the first baggie. It tested positive for cocaine. During booking, I examined Reynolds for signs of being under the influence of cocaine. He displayed no such symptoms.

I read Reynolds' Miranda rights to him from Form 238. After I read and explained those rights to him, Reynolds signed the attached form, agreeing to waive his rights and said, "Sure, I'll talk to you." He said that the drug was cocaine and he had purchased the drug the day before from a man he knows only by the name of "Jolly." He did not know where "Jolly" lived but he could always find him at a local bar called "Samy's", located at Thorpe and Walnut Street, in Orange.

Reynolds described "Jolly" as a male white, 30-35 years, 5-9", 175 lbs, black hair. He said he paid $20 for the bag. The empty bags that I found under the seat were old. Reynolds said that he had taken the drug the night before, at about 6:00 p.m. He said he uses cocaine about three to four times a week and has been doing so for about three months.

Reynolds was booked for violation of CVC section 22104 and California H&S Code section 11350 and was held for $25,000.00 bail. Case closed by arrest.

The following QR code is intended to invite realism into the investigatory and report writing process. It is an opportunity to act as if you are actually a police officer, probation or parole officer, social worker and/or any other position in criminal justice. Develop a plan of action and write the subsequent report from the perspective of an individual in that particular position.

Burglary Scenario - http://youtu.be/sO6unvMh9LE

Plan of action

_____
_____
_____
_____

Investigation

_____
_____
_____
_____

Report

_____
_____
_____
_____
_____
_____
_____
_____
_____
_____
_____
_____
_____

The following QR code is intended to invite realism into the investigatory and report writing process. It is an opportunity to act as if you are actually a police officer, probation or parole officer, social worker and/or any other position in criminal justice. Develop a plan of action and write the subsequent report from the perspective of an individual in that particular position.

Neighbor Dispute - http://youtu.be/smEq5YI8jDo

Plan of action

_____
_____
_____
_____

Investigation

_____
_____
_____
_____

Report

_____
_____
_____
_____
_____
_____
_____
_____
_____
_____
_____
_____
_____
_____
_____

The following QR code is intended to invite realism into the investigatory and report writing process. It is an opportunity to act as if you are actually a police officer, probation or parole officer, social worker and/or any other position in criminal justice. Develop a plan of action and write the subsequent report from the perspective of an individual in that particular position.

Despondent Male - http://youtu.be/ZenjVDcr_r8

Plan of action

_____
_____
_____
_____

Investigation

_____
_____
_____
_____

Report

_____
_____
_____
_____
_____
_____
_____
_____
_____
_____
_____
_____
_____

The following QR code is intended to invite realism into the investigatory and report writing process. It is an opportunity to act as if you are actually a police officer, probation or parole officer, social worker and/or any other position in criminal justice. Develop a plan of action and write the subsequent report from the perspective of an individual in that particular position.

Child Abuse - http://youtu.be/ix9AiA9VXwM

Plan of action

_____
_____
_____
_____

Investigation

_____
_____
_____
_____

Report

_____
_____
_____
_____
_____
_____
_____
_____
_____
_____
_____
_____
_____
_____

The following QR code is intended to invite realism into the investigatory and report writing process. It is an opportunity to act as if you are actually a police officer, probation or parole officer, social worker and/or any other position in criminal justice. Develop a plan of action and write the subsequent report from the perspective of an individual in that particular position.

Drunk in Public - http://youtu.be/DE09Ig17lts

Plan of action

_____

_____

_____

_____

Investigation

_____

_____

_____

_____

Report

_____

_____

_____

_____

_____

_____

_____

_____

_____

_____

_____

_____

_____

_____

_____

The following QR code is intended to invite realism into the investigatory and report writing process. It is an opportunity to act as if you are actually a police officer, probation or parole officer, social worker and/or any other position in criminal justice. Develop a plan of action and write the subsequent report from the perspective of an individual in that particular position.

Petty Theft - http://youtu.be/qL_sK1LBngg

Plan of action

_____
_____
_____
_____

Investigation

_____
_____
_____
_____

Report

_____
_____
_____
_____
_____
_____
_____
_____
_____
_____
_____
_____
_____
_____

The following QR code is intended to invite realism into the investigatory and report writing process. It is an opportunity to act as if you are actually a police officer, probation or parole officer, social worker and/or any other position in criminal justice. Develop a plan of action and write the subsequent report from the perspective of an individual in that particular position.

Stolen Vehicle - http://youtu.be/kH2nF1Cfx5E

Plan of action

_____
_____
_____
_____

Investigation

_____
_____
_____
_____

Report

_____
_____
_____
_____
_____
_____
_____
_____
_____
_____
_____
_____
_____
_____

The following QR code is intended to invite realism into the investigatory and report writing process. It is an opportunity to act as if you are actually a police officer, probation or parole officer, social worker and/or any other position in criminal justice. Develop a plan of action and write the subsequent report from the perspective of an individual in that particular position.

Lost Child - http://youtu.be/3YQUZUgNf2I

Plan of action

_____
_____
_____
_____

Investigation

_____
_____
_____
_____

Report

_____
_____
_____
_____
_____
_____
_____
_____
_____
_____
_____
_____
_____

The following QR code is intended to invite realism into the investigatory and report writing process. It is an opportunity to act as if you are actually a police officer, probation or parole officer, social worker and/or any other position in criminal justice. Develop a plan of action and write the subsequent report from the perspective of an individual in that particular position.

Stalker - http://youtu.be/jGcZJvWCu9M

Plan of action

_____
_____
_____
_____

Investigation

_____
_____
_____
_____

Report

_____
_____
_____
_____
_____
_____
_____
_____
_____
_____
_____
_____
_____